WHATEVER HAPPENED TO "SUPER JOE"?

WHATEVER HAPPENED TO "SUPER JOE"?

Catching Up With **45 Good Old Guys** from the **Bad Old Days** of the **Cleveland Indians**

Russell Schneider

GRAY & COMPANY, PUBLISHERS
CLEVELAND

Gray & Company, Publishers
www.grayco.com

Library of Congress Cataloging-in-Publication Data

Schneider, Russell J.
Whatever happened to Super Joe? : Catching Up With 45 Good Old Guys from the Bad Old Days of the Cleveland Indians / by Russ Schneider.
p. cm.
ISBN-13: 978-1-59851-027-0 (pbk.)
ISBN-10: 1-59851-027-4 (pbk.)
1. Cleveland Indians (Baseball team)—Biography—Anecdotes.
2. Baseball players—Ohio—Cleveland—Biography—Anecdotes.
I. Title.
GV865.A1S3333 2006
796.357'640977132—dc22   2006031519

Printed in the United States of America
10 9 8 7 6 5 4 3 2 1

This book is dedicated to many, beginning with my wife Kay, whose love, loyalty, understanding, patience, and support in all things personal and professional have been a blessing, and have made it possible for me to pursue my passion for sports, especially the wonderful game of baseball . . .

And to my late parents, my mother, Maybelle, the greatest Indians fan I've ever known, who never gave up hope that "next year" would soon arrive and be better, and my father, Robert, who eventually came to appreciate the game to which his wife and son were totally addicted . . .

And to all Tribe fans who have been waiting—often not so patiently—for their team to win a fourth World Series championship, which hasn't been achieved in six decades, despite coming ever so close in 1954, 1995, and 1997 . . .

And last, but certainly not least of all, to the good old guys from some of the bad old days of Indians baseball in Cleveland, whose memories of their careers, and reflections on the game as it was played back then and is played now, are recounted on the pages that follow.

The author wishes to thank Rob Lucas of Gray & Company, Publishers for his editorial assistance, and also Joe Simenic, a great Indians fan and baseball researcher, for his friendship and invaluable help in the preparation of the following stories.

CONTENTS

FOREWORD

Long ago Russ Schneider signed a contract to play professional baseball. So did the 45 then-young men featured in this book.

It can be assumed they, while from widely different backgrounds, shared a dream of making it to the faraway magical place called The Show, baseball's major leagues. And once there, of course, all the other dreams would come true.

Russ never made it to The Show. His career in the Indians organization was brief (personal analysis: "good field, not-so-good hitting catcher"). The others all did and played for the Indians.

The 45 were not superstars, although some had substantial careers, but that is the point made by the book's title and the reason for Russ's exhaustive work in supplying the answers. He was curious and knew many Indians fans would be, too.

By the nature of the sport, its long season, and the extensive coverage including all the television exposure, names of the players and associated recollections become part of the collective memory in the communities where they played. For long-time Indians fans, even players who were here briefly in insignificant roles can produce fond reflections. Where else do they remember Gomer (real name Harold) Hodge and Dirty Kurt Bevacqua?

In the years since he ended his long, productive career at the *Plain Dealer*—he prefers it not be called "retirement"—Russ produced a series of sports books, the total now reaching 13. Of these, 12 have been about baseball and the Indians, including *The Cleveland Indians Encyclopedia*. He has earned recognition as the leading historian of the Indians, the vigorous reporting and clear, nononsense prose that distinguished him at the *Plain Dealer* serving him well in his later-in-life role.

What he also has brought to this role is a lifetime attachment to baseball. One would be wary of describing it as a "love affair." Catchers are a rugged breed, the old-timers once capable of launching a stream of tobacco juice to emphasize a point, and they distain flowery poetic flights. They have observed baseball's harsh realities from behind a mask while doing its dirtiest job. And Russ on occasion can be among the sport's critics, sometimes in relation to what it has become in relation to what it was.

Yet if it could not be called a romance, his relationship with baseball started early and never stopped. Growing up, he played the other sports and even did some boxing, but baseball always was his favorite. He played baseball on the Cleveland sandlots, at West Tech High School, and during two hitches in the Marines. When his professional career with the Indians ended, he returned to the top Cleveland sandlot leagues for many more years as a catcher and then as a manager.

It has been said of many professional players, and some have said it themselves, that their passion for the sport was such that they would have played baseball for nothing if they no longer could be paid. How many ever did? Russ played for many years.

In middle age and beyond, he played slow-pitch softball when he and Kay were spending winters in Florida. Softball wasn't baseball but as close as he could come. He was well into his seventies when a succession of physical ailments finally closed down his career, undoubtedly by his own assessment prematurely.

All the years as a player is reflected in his empathy with those he writes about in this book. He is like the combat veteran with special insight in writing about war. Yet his obvious affection cannot be mistaken for hero worship. He respects the hard-earned skills required to play our most demanding team sport at its highest level but regards those who have not as heroes, but as humans, with all the quirks and failings the rest of us are heir to.

Looking back, it's clear his career as a reporter, which started him down a path he still follows, was launched by an offer he could not refuse.

By then, college, the Marines, pro baseball behind him, Russ was settling into a comfortable life with Kay and their children, two boys and a girl. He was doing well in his job, with the promise of better things ahead, in a field unrelated to sports.

The offer came from the *Plain Dealer* in 1964. It was for less money than he was making. Plus that, it would involve considerable travel, being away from his family.

But he would be the reporter covering the Indians.

Obviously family consultation was required. Serious thought given. But Kay, with some trepidation, agreed that her husband, feeling the way he did about baseball, couldn't pass up this opportunity.

So the boy who grew up dreaming he'd play for the Indians became the man who'd write about the Indians for 14 seasons before moving on to other assignments at the *Plain Dealer* in a career that would bring many honors, including induction into Cleveland's Journalism Hall of Fame and the Greater Cleveland Sports Hall of Fame. He did other things well at the *Plain Dealer*, especially investigative reporting, but writing about the Indians was central to his career in journalism and later to his books.

It is not necessary to ask *Whatever happened to* Russ Schneider. He never left. He still gets around town, gets to social and sports events. Since leaving the *Plain Dealer* in 1993, he's been active in many roles, including serving as chairman of the Ohio Boxing Commission and for years writing a column for the *Sun Newspapers* and, of course, producing his books.

He and Kay still live in Seven Hills, while spending winters in Lakeland, Florida. Sons Russell Jr. and Bryan and daughter Eileen, married to former Indians pitcher Eric Raich, live in the area. There are six grandchildren.

One of the many attractions of this book is the opportunity it offers the 45 former players to look back though the prism of all the years. The men they have become consider the young men they once were and offer evaluations of their careers and the much different times in which they played. The product is a wide range of thoughts, some surprising.

Russ was asked to take the same look back on his long association with baseball.

"Writing about baseball is the second best job in the world," he said. "The only one better is playing it."

—Bob August
Retired *Cleveland Press* Sports Editor

INTRODUCTION

They weren't always in the limelight, and their names and deeds weren't often headlined on the sports pages of the *Plain Dealer,* the old *Cleveland Press,* and the even older *Cleveland News.* But most of them are good old guys who played during the bad old days of baseball in Cleveland, when the Indians gave us so little to celebrate from the 1960s until the arrival of the "Era of Champions" in the mid-1990s.

Only seven times in those 25 consecutive seasons through 1994, when Jacobs Field opened, did the Indians win more games than they lost, and only once (1968) did they finish as high as third in the standings.

But despite those three-and-a-half decades of failure and frustration, there were players who not only deserve recognition for their efforts, but also are remembered as favorites, even when the Tribe's won-lost record was totally disappointing.

They weren't superstars—no disrespect intended—and if they were, nobody would be wondering where they have gone, what they are doing, and how do they assess all that has happened and is happening in major-league baseball today.

This, then, is a salute to them, 45 of the more than 1,600 men who have played at least one game for the Indians since the Cleveland franchise began in 1901.

To be sure, some are embittered, others simply disappointed, and several say they still can't understand why the Indians didn't fare better in those bad old days. Many are surprisingly outspoken in their criticism of major-league baseball's hierarchy and very much concerned about the future of the game most of them still love.

So, pull up a chair, kick back, and read as they comment on the

state of the Grand Old Game and reminisce and reflect on their careers, some of which were brief, others of which were more satisfying, and most of which would have been financially more lucrative
had the time and place been different.

JOE
CHARBONEAU

Outfielder, Designated Hitter, 1980–82

Best season: 1980, 131 games, .289 batting average, 23 home runs, 87 RBI

Indians career: 201 games, .266 avg., 29 home runs, 114 RBI

There was a book written about him, even a song, all of which should have thrilled Joe Charboneau, then a 25-five-year-old outfielder who won the American League Rookie of the Year award and was living his boyhood dream.

But, "To tell you the truth," Charboneau said as he reflected on his brief major-league career, "all that stuff embarrassed me . . . the nickname, the book, the song, the stories. I just wanted to play ball; I wasn't interested in a lot of publicity."

As it turned out, the career of "Super Joe"—as he came to be known to fans of the Indians—flamed out almost as quickly as it peaked. And peak it did. He batted .289 with 23 homers and 87 RBI in 1980. Then injuries that required back operations in 1981 and 1982 all but ended his career.

"After I hurt my back the first time, I never got rid of the pain, and I never got my swing back.

"I still have pain, though not as bad as when I played. I can only run maybe half speed, else my back will go out. I don't swing a bat. If I took a round in the batting cage, it would really hurt. I can play golf, but it's painful and I have to limp around the course."

Ah, but back in 1980, before he lost his swing and his power, Super Joe really was super, although, if he had a choice, it would have been that the nickname had never been coined.

"I was never a big fan of that Super Joe stuff," said the one-time Super Joe. "In fact, I was kind of surprised the first time I heard it."

A book, titled *Super Joe: The Life and Legend of Joe Charboneau*, followed. It was co-written by sportswriters Burt Graeff and Terry Pluto, who covered the Indians for the *Cleveland Press* (now defunct) and the *Cleveland Plain Dealer*, respectively.

Charboneau said the book is an "easy read with plenty of fun stuff in it, though a lot of the stories are only minimally true, some are greatly exaggerated, and others were never true to begin with."

Charboneau attributes their source to "buddies of mine who came in from California, got to drinking beer with some of the writers, and made up a lot of stuff."

Among the anecdotes: Charboneau opened beer bottles with his eye socket, ate cigarettes, drank beer with a straw through his nose, and once pulled an aching tooth and fixed his broken nose with a pair of pliers—and a shot of whiskey.

"It was all crazy stuff, but the truth is, I did get a lot of play from them. Every city I went to, the stories got bigger and bigger, and even different," he said.

"But I never brought them up, or encouraged the guys to write those things, and I really don't want to even talk about them now."

There also was a song that started with the lyrics, "Who's the newest guy in town? / Go Joe Charboneau. / Turns the ballpark upside down. / Go Joe Charboneau. / Who's the one to keep our hopes alive, straight from seventh to the pennant drive? / Raise your glass, let out a cheer for Cleveland's Rookie of the Year!"

Charboneau and his wife, Cynthia, whom he married in 1977, make their home in North Ridgeville, Ohio. They raised two children, a son, Tyson, born in 1979, and a daughter, Dannon, born in 1981.

Charboneau signed with the Philadelphia Phillies, who selected

"To tell you the truth, all that stuff embarrassed me . . . the nickname, the book, the song, the stories. I just wanted to play ball."

---

him in the second round of the secondary phase of the 1976 amateur draft. He received a $5,000 signing bonus in 1976, and his peak salary was $33,000 in 1981, in the wake of his "super" year.

"But, honest to God," Charboneau said, "I didn't play for the money. Not ever. Maybe that was dumb on my part because I had a family, but I loved to play baseball and I wanted to make the big leagues. The paycheck was just a bonus, really."

His Rookie of the Year season began when an injury sidelined Andre Thornton, making it possible for Charboneau to crack the starting lineup on April 11, 1980 in a 10-2 loss to California. He went 3-for-3, with a home run, launching the legend of Super Joe.

The highlight of the season came on June 28 in an 11-10 loss to the Yankees in New York. Charboneau blasted a home run into the third deck of Yankee Stadium, reached previously by only two players, Hall of Famer Jimmie Foxx and Frank Howard.

"I remember it like it was yesterday," said Charboneau. "Tom Underwood, a left-hander, was pitching for the Yankees. It was the first time I ever faced him, and I got ahead in the count, 3-and-1, and looked for a fastball in, which I got. I swung, and I never hit a ball better.

"As I was going around second base, I looked up to where the ball landed and thought to myself that I'd probably never hit another ball like that again. And I never did. It was a once-in-a-lifetime swing. Later they told me it was one of the three longest home runs ever hit in Yankee Stadium. Imagine that! Yankee Stadium, the 'House that Ruth built.'

"The whole thing was unbelievable. It seemed like the ball carried forever." The memory of it does for Charboneau.

Super Joe was super until the final three weeks of the season, when he got hurt. "It was something with my pelvis, and I didn't play anymore." He finished with 453 at-bats and 131 hits, of which 23 were homers. He won the rookie award easily, out-polling six other candidates. Charboneau was named on 102 ballots, more than doubling the 40 votes received by runner-up Dave Stapleton, an outfielder for Boston.

Unfortunately—for Charboneau and the Indians—his glory days ended when the season ended, ultimately attributable, he believes, to his back injuries.

"I realized early on that I probably didn't have as much talent as a lot of other guys and I had to play harder, which may be the reason I got hurt. I wasn't really a good outfielder; I didn't have a good arm, and I didn't steal a lot of bases. So I had to play harder, which I did. I played as hard as I could."

It was the following spring training, 1981, that Charboneau hurt his back sliding into second base head first. "It had rained that morning, and I basically kind of stuck in the dirt," he said. "My legs kicked back over my head, and I knew I did something. I had a lot of pain, and foolishly I continued to play. But I didn't have the same swing, and I never got it back."

After 48 games with the Indians in 1981, Charboneau was hitting .210 with four homers and 18 RBI, and was demoted to Class AAA Charleston, West Virginia, where he wasn't much better.

When the season ended, Charboneau underwent the first of two operations on his back. He played only 22 games in 1982 and hurt his back again, this time running to first base, and had more surgery the following August. For all practical purposes his career was finished.

Charboneau was back in spring training with the Indians in 1983 but soon was returned to the minors for rehabilitation, which wasn't successful. He was released.

"I refused to let it end my career. I kept trying to get back to the big leagues," he said. But that didn't happen.

Charboneau did get a trial with Class AAA Hawaii in the Pittsburgh farm system, but it didn't last long. Later he played for several independent teams in the United States and one in Europe, even a couple of semi-pro teams. Finally, in 2000, Super Joe gave up and took his last swing as a professional.

Charboneau coached for several teams in the independent Frontier League, and also, since 1991 he has operated "Joe Charboneau Baseball" in Twinsburg, Ohio, giving lessons and doing coaching clinics.

"Sure, I have a lot of regrets, but no complaints about anybody, and no bitterness. I always knew an injury could happen and, for me, it did. Somebody wrote an article about me in 1980, and I said all I really wanted to do was stay healthy. But I didn't."

And so ended—for Charboneau, the Indians, and their fans, much too soon—the legend of Super Joe.

CORY
SNYDER

Outfielder, Shortstop, Third Baseman, 1986–90

Best season: 1988, 142 games,
.272 batting average, 26 home runs,
75 RBI

Indians career: 657 games,
.245 avg., 115 home runs, 340 RBI

Cory Snyder and his wife, Tina, whom he married in 1985, are back at their adopted home in Mapleton, Utah, not far from Provo, where they both graduated from Brigham Young University. They are raising their six children in their strong Mormon faith.

Snyder's dedication to his religious principles often caused him problems with teammates and team officials during his nine-year major-league career. It was especially difficult for Snyder during his five seasons with the Indians, which began two years after he was the fourth player selected in the 1984 amateur draft.

An outstanding shortstop and two-time All-American at BYU, Snyder was a member of the 1984 United States Olympic team. He was an outfielder and sometimes third baseman/shortstop with the Tribe from 1986 until 1990, when he was traded to the Chicago White Sox. He later played briefly for Toronto, San Francisco, and Los Angeles through 1994, when his career ended—prematurely, he insists—at the age of 32.

It was with "some bitterness"—some of which obviously re-mains—that Snyder left professional baseball, though it did not end his love for the game.

"I felt I could still play, but it wasn't the same," he said. "I'd lost my edge, my desire. A lot of it was that I felt I was being pushed out."

When pressed to elaborate, Snyder said much of his disenchantment dated back to when he was with the Dodgers in 1994, the season that was aborted in August when the Major League Baseball Players Association went on strike.

"When my contract expired [at the end of 1994] and I became a free agent, the Dodgers weren't interested in keeping me . . . they let a lot of us go," he said.

Snyder tried to find another team that wanted him, but none was interested—except possibly on the minor-league level. "I'm not saying I was blackballed, but I think the fact that I'd been the player rep [with the Dodgers] and had been very involved with the Players Association didn't help my situation," he said.

Some of his bitterness also is directed toward the Players Association. "In retrospect, I regret being involved as much as I was back then. I didn't think [the union] took care of us the way they should have. I told them, 'Everything we did [in 1994] was because we thought it was right, and we wound up getting screwed.' The clubs took back the superstars and let the rest of us, the middle-of-the-road guys, go."

During his five years in Cleveland, Snyder established himself as one of baseball's best young power hitters, and in 1987 he and Joe Carter were pictured on the April 6 cover of *Sports Illustrated*. They were called the stars of the team—the Indians—that was favored to win the American League pennant.

Of course, that didn't happen; the Tribe finished seventh (again) in 1987 and was never a pennant contender until 1994.

Snyder's peak salary with the Indians was $700,000 in 1990, the year his once-promising career in Cleveland ended. He was traded on December 4 to the White Sox, who dealt him on July 14, 1991, to Toronto, which released him at the end of that season. He signed with and played for the Giants in 1992, after which he was granted free agency again and signed with the Dodgers.

It was during his time with the White Sox that Snyder's career began to spiral downhill.

"Looking back at it, I realize I tried too hard to please other people; I wasn't myself," he said. "I think it's something that happens to a lot of guys. If you start to struggle a little bit and you go to a new team, you get a new hitting coach and, instead of him working with what you have, he wants to change you. If the hitting coach had let me do what I had been doing—and what I had been doing OK—I think I would have been all right."

Instead, Snyder hit .188 in 50 games for the White Sox, and was even worse in Toronto, where he finished the season batting .143 in 21 games for the Blue Jays. Again, he was released.

Despite his initial unwillingness to identify the Chicago hitting coach, Snyder said it was Walt Hriniak. "He insisted on changing me. He thought my mechanics were all messed up and figured he had to revamp my whole swing to hit a certain way, and I just couldn't. With Hriniak it was his way or the highway."

Snyder joined the Giants as a minor-league free agent in 1992, made the major-league team, and seemed to be launching a comeback. He hit .269 with 14 homers in 124 games while playing every position except pitcher and catcher.

However, when the season ended, the Giants chose not to match the Dodgers' $3-million, two-year offer. Snyder returned to his hometown team (he and his wife both grew up in southern California), but it wasn't a good move.

"It turned out to be the end for me," he said. "Oh, I considered trying to hang on, but the desire was gone. Too many things in the game had changed. I always loved baseball, still do, but I didn't like being away from my family so much, and I also didn't like so many of the things that were happening . . . steroids and some of the things that go on when you're on the road, away from home.

"I was raised a Mormon, and I am still a Mormon. I don't swear and I don't drink. I didn't even want to be seen in a bar. That probably was the hardest thing about baseball for me, having so much in front of me, so much of the temptations, the drinking, the drugs, the carousing on the road, and having to sit there and see it, and be around it every single day. It was hard because it made you feel like you weren't part of the team, because you weren't doing those kinds of things.

"I really believe some of that stuff kind of got me traded by Cleveland because I didn't do the things that a lot of guys were doing. When John McNamara was our manager [in 1990] he accused me of not being a team player because, when we were on the road, I didn't hang out the way other guys did; he blamed me because, after the games, I just went back to my hotel room. I felt like they wanted me to go out with the guys.

"My attitude was, I was a professional and I wanted to do what was best for me to play baseball. Just to go out and stay out late, even though I wasn't drinking or doing any of the other stuff, I knew wasn't good for me. I was married, and I had more respect for my wife [than] to do those things."

Snyder also was critical of the way baseball handled the steroids and drug issues during the years he played in the major leagues.

"[Steroids] have been in the game for a long time. I know that. When I played it wasn't something that was openly talked about, as it is now. Now you see guys on TV who were in Triple-A saying, 'I've got to do something to compete against guys in the big leagues,' and they've got to decide if they are going to start taking them [steroids] or just go on the way they're going. It's a hard decision because so many guys are on them. It's almost like kids are being forced to do it, which is the worst part of all.

"I don't think the owners were bothered by it, because they wanted guys to hit 70 home runs. It also bothers me that the Players Association didn't do anything until they were forced to do so. They also knew what was happening and, in my opinion, let it go on for way too long.

"Like the Barry Bonds thing. He's breaking all those [home run] records but he didn't do it naturally. Certainly his records are tainted. Granted, he still has to go up there and hit the ball. But all the records of the guys he beat, and will beat . . . [those guys] didn't do it with steroids."

Snyder admitted there were Indians players who used steroids during his five seasons in Cleveland but declined to name them. "It's not my business anymore," he said.

Cory and Tina are raising their six children in the same strong Mormon faith they both live by. The children are daughters Ashley, born in 1990; Amberly, 1991; Aubrey, 1998; and Autumn, 2000; and sons Justin (J.C.), 1993, and Taylor, 1995. Snyder coaches his sons' baseball teams. In 2004, Justin's team, the Utah Stars, almost won the Youth Class AAA World Series tournament in Overland Park, Kansas, finishing second among 93 teams.

Snyder, who's in the real estate business in Mapleton, hasn't entirely given up his playing career. "A few years ago I played in a professional softball league and enjoyed it, except that after you've played at the level I did, it's more fun than competitive, and I have always enjoyed competition. I've found that the toughest thing I've had to do [since leaving professional baseball] is to replace the level of competition."

He also plays golf—he has a scratch handicap—and occasionally plays in a celebrity professional tournament. "I've won some money [in golf]—not a bunch, but some—but mainly I play for the competition."

Which led to a final question: Would he want to go back to professional baseball in some capacity?

"It's like [former Indians second baseman] Duane Kuiper said a few years ago when I saw him at a Giants game. 'Once you've played the game, you never get over missing it,' and he's right. Despite all the bad things, I confess I do miss being involved."

Which is why Snyder returned to the Indians in 2006 as a spring training instructor in their minor-league camp, and plans—*hopes*, really—to continue "as long as they want me," he said.

"I don't miss the drinking and the cursing and the carousing, all the bad things that go on in the big leagues, but I really enjoy working with kids before they get to the big leagues."

KURT
BEVACQUA

Second Baseman, Third Baseman, First Baseman, Shortstop, Outfielder, 1971–72

Best season: 1971, 55 games, .204 batting average, 3 home runs, 13 RBI

Indians career: 74 games, .186 avg., 4 home runs, 121 RBI

Kurt Bevacqua was not one of the best players to wear an Indians uniform, but he certainly was among the most interesting.

He was appropriately named "Dirty Kurt," not because he was considered to be a dirty player, but because his uniform was usually one of the team's dirtiest, the primary reason being that he played the game with such great intensity.

Neither should it be construed that, because of the brevity of his career with the Tribe, Dirty Kurt was not a good player. It's just that he didn't become one until after he left Cleveland, one of the eight times he was traded or sold during the 15 years he played in the major leagues.

The sometimes infielder/outfielder/DH, whose best position in the field arguably was second base, distinguished himself as a pinch-hitting specialist. Bevacqua also was one of the game's best bench jockeys. According to Bevacqua, bench jockeying is—or was—an "art form" in which outrageous insults are aimed at opposing players for the purpose of disrupting their concentration, especially when they're batting in clutch situations.

"But now it's a lost art," he said, "because everybody is buddy-

buddy, not like the way it was when I played. Now you have guys who play against each other who used to be teammates and they—or their wives—are good friends. Another reason is that so many guys who have the same agent play on different teams. And maybe the biggest reason is that everybody is a businessman, because everybody in the game is making so much money.

"I used to love to insult a guy . . . get under his skin . . . get him, you know, pissed off so he'd be thinking about how much he hated me instead of thinking about what he should be thinking about.

"I was good [as a bench jockey] and I knew it because so many guys hated me," said Bevacqua. "What the hell. I should have been good. I spent eight years of my career on the bench. I had a lot of practice."

He was so good, in fact, that a recently published "book of lists" that included the 12 best bench jockeys in the history of baseball ranked Bevacqua fourth—the top-rated player on the list. Ahead of him, one through three, were Billy Martin, Earl Weaver, and Bill Rigney, all former managers. (Behind Bevacqua, numbers 5 through 12 were Leo Durocher, Eddie Stanky, Jimmy Dykes, Frankie Frisch, Lefty Gomez, Whitey Ford, John McGraw, and Dizzy Dean. All but Gomez and Ford were managers.)

Other than his talent for angering opponents with his insults, Bevacqua also was considered one of the game's best pinch hitters, especially during his service with Pittsburgh (twice), the Milwaukee Brewers, and San Diego (twice).

"Being a pinch hitter is one of the toughest jobs in baseball. Not only is it usually unrewarding, it also is very stressful. You're always under pressure. But I loved it, and I was proud of my ability as a pinch hitter," said Bevacqua.

"I felt like a relief pitcher coming out of the bullpen to get a guy out, or to pitch an inning with the game on the line, like Mariano Rivera coming in to save the game. I always felt I was in that kind of a situation when I pinch hit, and it didn't matter if the pitcher was left-handed or right-handed.

"I approached it this way—that I wasn't facing one of the best

"I was good [as a bench jockey]. I should have been good. I spent eight years of my career on the bench. I had a lot of practice."

---

pitchers in the game, but that the pitcher was facing the best pinch hitter in the game. Maybe it was just a little psychological game I played in my head, but it worked, and I really believed in myself.

"When I played for Jerry Coleman when he managed the Padres [in 1980], he said there were a couple of times he almost had me pinch hit for [Hall of Famer] Dave Winfield," said Bevacqua. "He said the reason he didn't was because he was afraid he'd get [hanged] by the owner and the media if he did. And Winnie would have been more than slightly pissed off, too."

Bevacqua, who was drafted by Cincinnati in 1967 after he was previously picked by the New York Mets and Atlanta, made it to the big leagues with the Indians when they acquired him in a May 8, 1971, trade. His career with the Tribe ended after two seasons, when he was dealt to the Royals.

"I hated Cleveland," he said. "I wasn't burning up the league, but I was doing OK, and I liked playing for [manager] Alvin Dark."

He batted .204 in 55 games, mostly at second base.

"If Dark hadn't been fired I probably would have liked it better. But as soon as [Ken] Aspromonte came in [replacing Dark in 1972], I went back to the pine."

The highlight of Bevacqua's career probably was in 1984, when the Padres played Detroit in the World Series. It was his three-run, fifth-inning homer off Dan Petry that gave San Diego its only victory, 5-3, in the second game. Bevacqua also homered in Game Five, won by the Tigers, 8-4. He batted .412 (7-for-17) in the Series.

Bevacqua's last season in baseball was 1985, with the Padres. He retired with a .236 career batting average—but wasn't out of work for long. "I went home to San Diego, and within two weeks I was working [in broadcasting] for NBC Sports," he said.

Later, after NBC lost its contract with major-league baseball, Bevacqua worked for a San Diego television station doing Padres pre- and post-game shows which, he said, "opened the doors to a lot of opportunities for me." He subsequently founded a company called "Major League Systems" that sells after-market products to car dealers.

Bevacqua and his third wife, Cynthia, live on the first tee at the LaCosta Country Club where he now "works" (his word) daily at improving his golf handicap, which at the time of this interview was "down around six or seven."

"I have to tell you," he said, "I have a pretty good life. I couldn't be much happier than I am right now—not even if I were still playing baseball."

JAMES (MUDCAT)
GRANT

Pitcher, 1958–64

Best season: 1961, 35 games, 15-9 won-lost record, 0 saves, 3.86 ERA

Indians career: 227 games, 67-63 won-lost record, 8 saves 4.09 ERA

The trade—some considered it a "giveaway"—that sent Mudcat Grant from the Indians to Minnesota in 1964 is a perfect case history of the financial insecurity that plagued the Cleveland franchise in the "bad old days." That would be the era that began in the early-1960s and continued into the mid-1990s, marked by losing teams and small crowds.

Grant, who grew up in the Tribe farm system after he signed as an 18-year-old amateur free agent in 1954—his "bonus," he said, was a "handshake"—had become one of the team's best young pitchers from the time he made his major-league debut in 1958.

He showed promise of being so good, in fact, that the Indians apparently believed they would be unable to afford his salary and, thus dealt him (OK, *gave* him) away to the Twins on June 15, 1964. At the time the franchise was owned by William R. Daley, and Gabe Paul was general manager.

In exchange for Grant, the Indians received Lee Stange, a pitcher who would continue to have an undistinguished career the next two seasons in Cleveland; George Banks, an equally undistinguished third baseman/outfielder; and an undisclosed amount of cash (don't forget the money!).

Fast forward to the present.

Grant, while dealing with several infirmities, including diabetes, arthritis, and knee problems, stays active in a variety of charitable endeavors. Many of them involve African American athletes on behalf of children around the country. Among them is one he founded, the "Thirteen Black Aces Foundation," which comprises the 13 African American pitchers who won 20 games in the major leagues.

Mudcat, of course, is one of them. The others: Vida Blue, Al Downing, Bob Gibson, Dwight Gooden, Ferguson Jenkins, Sad Sam Jones, Don Newcombe, Mike Norris, J.R. Richard, Dave Stewart, Dontrelle Willis, and Earl Wilson.

"We produce products—lithographs, posters, and the like, including a book that's being written [by Grant]—that are sold to raise money for charitable organizations."

Grant also heads a marketing company, BGAT Slugger, that, he said, "holds baseball clinics, among other fund-raising events . . . anything we can do to influence kids and motivate them in terms of education."

In addition, Grant serves in various capacities with the Negro League Hall of Fame, Baseball Assistance Team, and Major League Baseball Alumni Association, among others, in support of former players who are not well off financially.

Until he was slowed by physical problems, Grant also was active in the entertainment business. As a singer and dancer, he and his group toured the country as "Mudcat and the Kittens" and in 2004 gave concerts in both Europe and the U.S.

Grant and his second wife, Gertrude, whom he met in Vienna, Austria, and married in 1975, make their home in the Los Angeles area. He has five children from his first marriage, including a son, James Timothy Grant III, who lives in the Cleveland area.

"I loved the Indians and I always thought they loved me, until—apparently—they couldn't afford me," said Grant, whose 14-year major league won-lost record was 145-119 with a 3.63 earned run average in 571 games.

"I loved the Indians and I always thought they loved me until—apparently— they couldn't afford me."

"Cleveland was the only place I liked almost as much as Lacoochie," which was Mudcat's hometown in Florida.

He still harbors a painful memory of the day he was dealt to Minnesota. "The Twins were in [Cleveland] when I was traded, but nobody told me about it. I went to my locker in the clubhouse and there was nothing there. It was bare. I asked the clubbie [clubhouse attendant], and he said, 'Your stuff is in the Twins' clubhouse.' I asked him, 'What's it doing over there?' and he said, 'You've been traded to Minnesota.' "He's the one who told me. Nobody from the front office, or [Indians interim manager George Strickland] bothered to tell me.

"I went to the Twins' clubhouse and, sure enough, my stuff was there. Apparently they made the deal the night before. I didn't know what to say to anybody, so I didn't [say anything]. I just got dressed and walked out on the field. Some fans asked me, 'What are you doing in that uniform?' and all I could say was that I got traded."

Grant flourished with the Twins (in 1964–67) and went on to pitch for the Los Angeles Dodgers (1968), Montreal and St. Louis (1969), and Oakland and Pittsburgh (1970–71).

With the Twins in 1965 he became the first African American pitcher to win 20 games in the American League (when his record was 21-7), and pitched them into the World Series. He became an ace reliever the last two years of his career and was credited with 53 saves, including 24 with the Athletics in 1970. He is one of only six pitchers in major league history to win 20 games in one season and save 20 victories in another.

Ironically, just as it was financial trouble that caused the Indians to trade Grant, he ran into similar problems in Minnesota with owner Calvin Griffith. After leading the Twins to their first pennant after the franchise's move to Minneapolis, Grant asked for a $4,500 raise, a modest sum by today's standard, but was promptly rejected.

"Calvin asked me, 'Mud, how much was your share from the World Series?' I said it was $4,500, and he said, 'Well, if I give you $2,000, that'll be $6,500 more than you made last year.'

"I told him to shove it and that I was going home to Lacoochie. He told me, 'We can negotiate,' but he kept telling me he couldn't pay me what I wanted so I got a cab—we were in Florida for spring training at the time—and I went home. That convinced the Twins I was serious, and they called me back and gave me a $13,000 raise."

Grant didn't say how much that boosted his salary, but six years later, in 1971 with Pittsburgh (his final season in baseball), he was paid $82,000, a career high.

That also was five years before free agency came into being, when players gained the right to sell their services to the highest bidders. Soon thereafter most became millionaires.

"I'm not bitter that I wasn't around when the big money came in," said Grant. "But I hope players today realize that one of the reasons they're doing so well is because of what we did in the past. Our hard work and sacrifices helped them get where they are."

After he retired as a player, Grant worked for the Indians in community relations and also was a member of their broadcasting team from 1972 into the early 1980s. He later did some television work for the Dodgers and the Athletics.

Looking back, Grant said, "The high point of my major-league career took place before it even started. It was the night I signed a major-league contract with the Indians in 1958, and I thought about all the African American players who had preceded me . . . Jackie Robinson and Larry Doby and Luke Easter and Don Newcombe and Monte Irvin and Joe Black and so many others.

"We didn't have a telephone in my home [in Lacoochie] at that time, so I wrote my mother a letter and told her, 'Mom, I made it!'—even though it took three days for her to get it."

GOMER
HODGE

Second Base, Third Base, First Base, 1971

Best (only) season: 1971, 80 games, .205 batting average, 1 home run, 9 RBI

Indians career: 80 games, .205 avg., 1 home runs, 9 RBI

The years have not been kind to Harold "Gomer" Hodge since his departure—actually, his unwilling "retirement"—from professional baseball, after he was fired as a minor-league coach for the Montreal Expos in 2001.

"They never told me why; they just let me go," Hodge said from his home in Rutherfordton, North Carolina, where he was born and raised, and was a star baseball, basketball, and football player at Spindale High School in the early 1960s. Rutherfordton is about 60 miles west of Charlotte.

"I'd like to get back in [base]ball, but I can't because of my health," said Hodge. He has been on total disability for several years, primarily because of problems with his back and other ailments. "I can't do much of anything anymore."

At the time of our interview, Gomer was in the early stages of Amyotrophic Lateral Sclerosis (ALS), also known as "Lou Gehrig Disease."

Though his given name was Harold, Hodge was nicknamed "Gomer" by his minor-league teammates because "some of my northern buddies thought I sounded like that guy on television,

Gomer Pyle," he said. Gomer Pyle was a character on the old Andy Griffith television show, played by actor-singer Jim Nabors, who later starred in his own TV show, *Gomer Pyle, U.S.M.C.*

Though his major-league career consisted of only one season (1971), Hodge is still a favorite of Tribe fans of that era because, well, primarily because he was such a charismatic, pleasant, unpretentious, and extremely likable character.

He played first, second, and third base. "But my best position," Gomer said, "was hitting."

Hodge's popularity took off after back-to-back pinch-hitting appearances. On Opening Day in Detroit, April 6, 1971, Gomer singled for a run against the Tigers' Mickey Lolich. In the Tribe's next game, the home opener in Cleveland against Boston on April 8, Gomer pinch-doubled and scored the Indians' first run in the eighth inning. He remained in the game at second base and, in the bottom of the ninth, delivered a two-out, two-run single for a 3-2 Tribe victory.

Three days later, in the Indians fourth game, Hodge came through again as a pinch hitter, this time with an eighth-inning double as the Indians again beat Boston, 7-2.

It gave Gomer four hits in his first four official at-bats, after which he chortled in a post-game interview, "Gollee, fellas, I'm hitting 4.000," a remark that will always remain his legacy.

Unfortunately, Hodge's—and the Indians'—season went into rapid decline thereafter, though Gomer enjoyed one more day in the limelight. On September 3, he smashed a home run, his only one in the major leagues, in Boston over Fenway Park's infamous left-field wall, again as a pinch hitter.

When the season ended with the Indians mired in sixth place, tying a franchise record for futility—102 losses—Hodge, whose batting average had shrunk from "4.000" to .205, was demoted to Portland of the Class AAA Pacific Coast League.

"They said they wanted me to go down and concentrate on playing one position," said Gomer. "After a little while they asked me to be a player-coach, and I knew right away they didn't have any plans to call me back, but that was OK. I figured if they thought enough of me to want me to be a player-coach, that was pretty good."

He was right. Hodge remained a minor-league player-coach and eventually a manager in the Indians farm system through 1976, when he was fired. He went home to Rutherfordton, where he helped his father on the farm and tried to forget about baseball.

But in 1981, Bob Quinn, then the Indians' farm director, called and asked Hodge if he wanted to manage Waterloo, Iowa, in the Class A Midwest League. "I sure did," said Gomer. "But first I asked Quinn why they fired me, and he said, 'Because you had a horse-bleep record, didn't you?' which I did. All I could figure was that he must have thought I got smarter working on my dad's farm."

Maybe he did. He won the Manager of the Year award in the Midwest League in 1981 and 1983. It also was in Waterloo that Hodge met his first wife, Deborah, though he was reluctant to talk about her, even to mention her by name.

"We were married almost twenty years . . . She told me I'd never catch her cheating on me, but I did and she left me with about $20,000 in bills," he said. They had two children, son Nicholas and daughter Morgan. Hodge and his second wife, Linda, a probation officer in Rutherfordton, were married in 2002.

Gomer went on to work in the minor leagues in various positions as a manager, coach, and hitting instructor for the Milwaukee Brewers, Boston, and Montreal. He even coached teams in Australia and Mexico until back and hip problems curtailed his physical activities. He was forced to retire in 2001.

The highlight of his career? "There were lots of them," he said, somewhat surprisingly considering that he spent only one year in the major leagues. (It took him eight seasons in the minors to get there, and he spent three more as a player-coach in the Indians farm system from 1972 to 1974.)

"My biggest thrill was when [manager] Alvin Dark called me into his office during spring training on April 3, 1971," he said. "I remember the date because that was my 27th birthday and I was afraid he was going to tell me I was going back to the minors. Instead he told me I made the team. It was the best birthday present I ever got.

"When people ask me how many home runs I hit in the big leagues and I say one, they laugh. But then I tell them, 'I bet you wish you'd been able to hit one,' and they don't laugh any more. I hit my home run over the Green Monster in Boston. It wasn't a game winner, but it was a home run . . . it sure was. And those four pinch hits were pretty good, too.

"I still have a fan club in Cleveland. It's not too big anymore, but I still get letters from fans who want my autograph. I always sign 'Gomer' for them, but I'm Harold to everybody down here."

Something else that Gomer remembers with pride, though it didn't happen during his playing days, was a scouting assignment in the winter of 1992–93 that he made while working for the Expos.

"They sent me to the Dominican Republic with another of their scouts to look at some players," said Hodge. "I found a 17-year-old kid and told the Expos they should sign him. They did, and now he's in the big leagues. I get a thrill reading about how good he is."

That "kid" is Vladimir Guerrero, who became one of the best players in baseball, won the American League's Most Valuable Player award in 2004 as a member of the Los Angeles Angels, and signed a $12.5 million contract in 2005.

"I'd like to have a couple hundred of that [salary]," said Hodge, who made $13,500 (the major-league minimum) in 1971. "That [$13,500] is worth about one time at-bat today.

"I'm not bitter, just disappointed the way things turned out. Not because I didn't make a bunch of money, but because I love base-ball and I'd still like to be in it. If I sound like I'm sad, it's probably because I have a bad cold and my nose is all stuffed up.

"When I played it was because we loved the game, not for the money. And the guys who are making all the money now, when they come out of the game I guarantee they won't have enjoyed it as much as I did," said Gomer.

DAVE
LAROCHE

Pitcher, 1975–77

Best Season: 1975, 61 Games,
Won-Lost Record 5-3, 17 Saves,
2.19 ERA

Indians career: 135 games,
8-9 won-lost record, 42 saves,
2.51 ERA

Dave LaRoche pitched his final game in 1983 as a member of the New York Yankees, ending an illustrious 14-year major-league career, though it certainly didn't end his involvement—or his family's involvement—with baseball.

And though he spent only two-plus seasons with the Indians, "I had a great time in Cleveland," said LaRoche. He was elected the team's Man of the Year for 1975 and was the Tribe's only representative on the American League all-star team in 1976, the season he set a club record (at the time) with 21 saves in 61 appearances.

An ill-conceived trade that sent him to California in 1977 made clear, in retrospect, the ongoing financial problems that plagued the Indians at that time and which would continue for more than a decade.

"We weren't very good, and we didn't draw a lot of fans, but those we had were loyal," said LaRoche. "The only thing I didn't like about Cleveland was the old Stadium. Too bad they didn't tear it down and build a new park while I was still there."

LaRoche has remained in baseball as a coach at both the major- and minor-league levels, and also maintains a personal—OK, a *family*—interest in the game that he played for five major-league teams. While LaRoche himself is no longer in the limelight, there's no doubt baseball fans are aware of another "LaRoche"—and that possibly a second one will come along soon—thanks to the genes passed along by Dave and his wife Patty to their five children.

Their second oldest son, Adam, born in 1979, is one of the bright young stars in the National League. He was drafted by Atlanta in 2000, made it to the major leagues in 2004, and is the Braves first baseman, although, as he says, he's told manager Bobby Cox that he's available to pitch if the need arises.

"Adam has a good arm, throws hard, and has a real good curve and change-up, but he's also a good hitter," said Dave.

Another son, Andy, born in 1983, is a third baseman who was drafted by the Los Angeles Dodgers in 2002. He was voted the organization's player of the year in 2005 when he led all L.A. minor leaguers with 30 homers and 94 RBI at Class A Vero Beach and Class AA Jacksonville, earning a promotion to the Dodgers' 40-man roster in 2006.

A third son, Jeff, born in 1978, a left-handed pitcher like his dad, played pro baseball for seven years. He retired in 2004 to become a police officer in Vail, Colorado.

But that's not all. Patty and Dave, who make their home in Fort Scott, Kansas, have two daughters, Nanette and Nikki, whose abilities reflect their athletic bloodline. Patty was a better-than-average college softball shortstop, and both daughters went to college on athletic scholarships, Nanette in softball and volleyball, and Nikki in softball.

Dave LaRoche came to Cleveland in one of general manager Phil Seghi's best trades but left under unpleasant circumstances. He started his pro career as an outfielder. He was selected in the fifth round of the amateur draft by California in 1967, but switched to pitching in the minor leagues in 1968 when the Angels decided they liked his arm better than his bat.

They were right. LaRoche got to the major leagues in 1970 and soon became one of baseball's premier relievers. He compiled a 65-58 won-lost record and 3.53 earned run average in 647 games, all but 15 in relief, for California, Minnesota, the Chicago Cubs, the Indians, and the Yankees.

"Most of the time I was a closer, though it was different back then," said LaRoche. "Relievers didn't have defined roles as they do today. Teams had a left and right [handed] long man, a middle man, and a short man in the bullpen. If you were the short man, as I was most of the time, you'd come into the game in the sixth or seventh inning and stay as long as you were getting guys out. Now everybody is a specialist. I don't know if that's better than the way it was, but if you're a closer or short reliever as I was, it's a lot easier now."

LaRoche never really left the game after throwing his final pitch in 1983. Much of his involvement in baseball has to do with keeping track of sons Adam and Andy, though not as much as he'd like because he's still active himself.

LaRoche was a minor-league coach for three organizations from 1984 to 1988, then returned to the major leagues in 1989 as a coach for the Chicago White Sox under former California and Cleveland teammate Jeff Torborg. They were together with the White Sox for three seasons, and with the New York Mets for two more (1992–93). When Torborg was released by the Mets, LaRoche remained as their minor-league pitching coach in 1994.

He returned home in 1995 "to help Patty raise the boys"—and, of course, to help their development in baseball—while he coached the community college baseball team in Fort Scott the next five years.

"By then [2001] the boys were grown and going into pro ball themselves, so I did, too," said LaRoche. He went back to the minors as a coach for Kansas City in 2003 and 2004, and since 2005 has been the pitching coach for Toronto's team in the Class AA Eastern League.

Reflecting on his career with the Indians, LaRoche said, without rancor or great elaboration, "Too often back then [management] moved players for financial reasons, which hurt the team."

LaRoche's analysis was accurate. Money was the major factor in his being traded on May 11, 1977, to the Angels, the organization with which he began his professional career 10 years earlier.

As with so many deals that management of the Indians of that era felt compelled to make, groundwork for the deal was laid three months earlier, in February, prior to the start of spring training. LaRoche, who wasn't signed for the coming season, delivered through the media what general manager Phil Seghi considered an ultimatum. He was quoted as saying he wanted a five-year, guaranteed contract, or he'd declare himself a free agent at the end of the season.

Bear in mind, that was shortly after the advent of free agency in baseball—and also was shortly after the Indians had signed free-agent pitcher Wayne Garland to a $2.3 million, 10-year guaranteed contract.

Seghi reacted predictably. He promptly negotiated with LaRoche and signed him to a 1977 contract for a reported $85,000, a raise of about $17,000. The deal ensured the Indians keeping LaRoche for the season, or long enough to trade him—which Seghi did.

Forty-one days into the season, after LaRoche appeared in 13 games with a 2-2 record and four saves, he was sent back to the Angels in exchange for first baseman-outfielder Bruce Bochte, pitcher Sid Monge, and a reported $250,000. It was typical of the Indians' *modus operandi* of that era; they almost always insisted upon receiving money, along with players, in any deal they made.

When LaRoche joined the Angels, they signed him to a new contract, one that he said paid him a million dollars, guaranteed over five years. It was the same deal he'd sought but couldn't get from the Indians.

Thus ended the Indians career of LaRoche—and another chapter in the bad old days of Cleveland baseball.

MAX
ALVIS

Third Baseman, 1962–69

Best season: 1963, Man of the Year, 158 games, .274 batting average, 22 home runs, 67 RBI

Indians career: 951 games, .249 avg., 108 home runs, 361 RBI

Two weeks after Max Alvis reported to the Indians' minor-league spring-training camp in Daytona Beach, Florida in 1959, one of the coaches, former major-league outfielder Bob Kennedy, spoke to the 20-year-old rookie third baseman.

"'I've only seen you play a few games,'" Alvis related Kennedy's comments, "'but I'll tell you one thing right now, Max, and that is, if you don't make it to the big leagues I'm sure it won't be your fault.'

"It was one of the greatest compliments I ever received . . . something I'll never forget," said Alvis.

Obviously, Kennedy was right. After four minor-league seasons—(Class D) Selma, Alabama, 1959; (Class C) Minot, North Dakota, 1960; (Class AAA) Salt Lake City, 1961–62)—Alvis made it to the big leagues. He was the Indians' Opening Day third baseman in 1963.

At the time, general manager Gabe Paul advertised that Alvis and two other young prospects—center fielder Vic Davalillo and shortstop Tony Martinez—would be the cornerstone of an Indians dynasty. Unfortunately, Davalillo's career fell short of expectations after he suffered a broken arm when hit by a pitch in 1963 (though

"The highest salary I ever made was $30,000 in 1969. In those days you either took what [the owners] were offering or went home."

he went on to play 16 seasons in the major leagues with five other teams). And Martinez never made an impact, playing only briefly and not very well in 73 games over the next four seasons, and never reappeared in the major leagues.

But Alvis more than lived up to Paul's high hopes and Kennedy's prediction during his eight seasons in Cleveland. Max remained with the Tribe through 1969, during which he was voted the team's Man of the Year twice—in 1963 and 1967—and was a member of the American League All-Star team in 1965 and 1967.

It also was in 1967 that Alvis was overwhelmingly voted the most popular player—even ahead of Rocky Colavito—in the history of the franchise in a "Favorite Indians" contest conducted among the fans by the *Plain Dealer*.

After the Indians acquired Graig Nettles to play third base and had a young Buddy Bell waiting in the wings, Alvis was traded to the Milwaukee Brewers on April 4, 1970. He retired after one season with the Brewers, returned to his roots in Jasper, Texas (a small town of about eight thousand located about two and a half hours northeast of Houston), and eventually became president of the First National Bank of Jasper. Alvis has been with the bank since 1977, first as a loan officer, then vice-president and president.

"I guess you can say I got this job [as president of the bank] the same way I learned to play third base. You get enough bad hops and pretty soon you can handle them. I made enough mistakes at the bank and learned from them, too. Until then the only thing I knew about the banking business when I started was that I'd borrowed a good bit of money—but never loaned any." Now, as he said, "The buck stops at my desk. I'm the guy who signs off on all the loans we make."

Alvis's baseball career probably would have lasted longer—and been even better—but for a nearly fatal bout with spinal meningitis that struck him in 1964. It began on the Indians' flight from Minneapolis-St. Paul to Boston the night of June 25, after a game against the Minnesota Twins.

"I was feeling pretty good when we got on the plane. I'd had a good game, hit a couple of dingers [homers], and felt I was busting out the slump I'd been in. But, no sooner did we get off the ground then I got a headache, a very intense headache that kept getting progressively worse. I took a couple of aspirins but they didn't help, and by the time we got to our hotel in Boston it was so bad I couldn't sleep."

About three in the morning his roommate, catcher John Romano, called trainer Wally Bock, who examined Alvis and discovered he was running a high fever. Bock immediately took him to Sancta Maria Hospital where the illness was diagnosed as spinal meningitis.

"It was scary, although at the time I didn't know what meningitis was," said Alvis. "When they started telling me that people died from it, playing your next baseball game doesn't seem so important.

"Not only was I worried about myself, I was worried about my family and the team, even you guys," he quipped, referring to reporters who traveled with the Indians.

Alvis was hospitalized for almost a month, then spent a couple more weeks at home in Jasper. Though the doctor recommended that he not play again that season, Alvis rejoined the Indians in late August. He played the final six weeks, finishing with a .252 average, 18 homers, and 53 RBI in 107 games.

"At the time I wasn't concerned about the possibility of any aftereffects," said Alvis. "I thought I was over and done with it. But in retrospect, I soon realized I didn't have the same strength, the same stamina and endurance I'd had before I got sick. I remember that I was constantly changing bats, thinking maybe I should go to one that was lighter, but it didn't help.

"Before I got sick I worked hard and I wasn't intimidated by anything. But when I came back I really don't think I had the brute strength that I'd had, and I couldn't regain it. [Meningitis] did something to my system. I never had any other after effects that I know of, but I just wasn't as strong as I'd been before.

"Looking back at it, I know I wasn't the same, so maybe it did cut my career short."

Whatever, Alvis's performance on the field declined thereafter. When the Indians traded him to the Brewers, he played only 62 games in 1970, batted .183 with three homers, and hung up his spikes.

Prior to signing for a $40,000 bonus with the Indians in 1959 (the amateur draft was not in effect then) Alvis was, as he said, "a hard-nosed football player, the same way I played baseball. I wasn't a star, but I guess I was pretty good." He was a halfback/linebacker at the University of Texas and played in the Sugar Bowl after the Longhorns went 8-3 in 1958.

He and his wife, Frances Mae—better known as "Honey"—were married in 1958 and raised two sons, Max Jr. and David. (David played three years in the Indians' minor-league system as a first baseman in the early 1980s.) They have five grandchildren.

"I can't really pinpoint any one thing as the highlight of my baseball career," Alvis answered the obvious question. "I tell people that, in my case, just getting to the big leagues and playing professional baseball was a tremendous accomplishment. I never felt I was superstar material, though I believe I had a good career with the ability I had. I'm real proud of having done what I did.

"The highest salary I ever made was $30,000 in 1969. In those days you either took what [the owners] were offering or went home. I have no idea what I might be worth if I were playing today, but that's not important. I'm just happy with what I was able to do. I just wish I could have done it longer."

CHRIS
CHAMBLISS

First Baseman, 1971–74

Best season: 1972, 121 games, .292 batting average, 6 home runs, 44 RBI

Indians career: 404 games, .282 avg., 26 home runs, 152 RBI

It has been a long and frustrating journey for Chris Chambliss, a journey that began in 1987, after his 16th and final season as a major-league first baseman. And, because of his determination to achieve the same degree of success he did as a player, the journey will continue.

"I've made no secret of the fact that I want to manage in the big leagues, and I think I have paid, and still am paying my dues," he said. "I've interviewed a lot, but nothing has happened. I can't distinguish which [interviews] were just cursory . . . which of the clubs were just going through the motions to satisfy the commissioner that they were interviewing a minority candidate. I think too much of that goes on, although there were some interviews that I thought were great. But nothing has come of them."

And he also said again, lest there be any misunderstanding, "My aspirations are still the same, and I believe I am ready [to manage in the big leagues]."

Chambliss added, and which his resume tends to verify, "I am still accumulating experience and knowledge" since retiring as Atlanta's first baseman.

He was a major-league coach for Cincinnati from 2004 to 2006. Prior to that he was a coach for the Yankees (1987–88, 1996–2000), St. Louis (1993–95), and the New York Mets (2003). He managed in the minor leagues at the Class AAA and AA levels for five years (1989–92, 2001) for the Detroit, Atlanta, and Florida organizations, during which he won two Manager of the Year awards (1990, 1991), as well as being named Minor-League Manager of the Year by the *Sporting News* (1991).

Chambliss's credentials as a player are equally impressive. He was selected No. 1 in the country by the Indians in the January 1970 amateur draft. He'd previously been picked twice by the Reds, in 1967 and 1968, but declined their offers to continue his college studies at UCLA.

The Indians gave Chambliss, then 22, a $35,000 signing bonus, which proved to be a good investment, although they—unfortunately—traded him away four years later.

Chambliss won unprecedented back-to-back Rookie of the Year awards in his first two seasons of professional baseball, the first in 1970, when he led the Class AAA American Association with a .342 batting average at Wichita, Kansas, and the second in the American League in 1971, when he batted .275 for the Tribe. But then, because the Indians were in dire need of pitching, they included Chambliss in an ill-conceived, seven-player deal with the Yankees on April 26, 1974.

He went on to play for New York through 1979, and for the Braves from 1980 to 1986, finishing his active career with a .279 average with 185 home runs and 972 RBI.

Chambliss had a simple, though somewhat unusual explanation for his hitting prowess. "As a young boy," he said, "I played a game with a broom stick and bottle caps, similar to what kids say today about stick ball. We used a bottle cap like it was a ball, threw it like a Frisbee, and the batter got one swing to get a hit or make an out. I don't know if that's what made me a good hitter, but I'm sure it didn't hurt."

"If you can hit a baseball that's going 95 miles an hour, steroids won't help you hit it better. Maybe farther, but you still have to make contact."

The son of a Navy chaplain, Chambliss was born in Dayton, Ohio, and grew up in California. He and his wife, Audrey, whom he married in 1973, have a son, Russell, who played minor-league baseball in the Yankees farm system from 1997 to 1999.

It was in New York that Chambliss had his best seasons, especially in 1976, when his walk-off home run on October 14 won the pennant for the A.L. East Division champion Yankees in the ALCS playoff against Kansas City, winner of the A.L. West.

It was one of the most dramatic home runs in the history of baseball, the highlight of Chambliss's career, and it gave the Yankees their first pennant in 12 years. It also was their first of three consecutive pennants—probably not coincidentally—with Chambliss as their first baseman. Chambliss hit the game-winning homer against the Royals in the deciding game of the ALCS. It came on Mark Littell's first pitch in the bottom of the ninth, breaking a 6-6 tie the Royals had fashioned in the eighth on a three-run homer by George Brett.

The 55,000-plus fans who filled Yankee Stadium to capacity erupted in a frenzy. They poured out of the stands and onto the field, forcing Chambliss to literally fight his way around the bases. He never stepped on home plate after his homer landed in the right-field stands.

"The fans were on the field, hundreds of them, and I was basically just trying to get around the bases and get back to the dugout," Chambliss recalled.

As he neared second base, the bag had already been ripped from the ground, but before it was carried away Chambliss reached over and touched it with his right hand. When he got to the shortstop's position, he ran into a fan and fell, picked himself up and, as he said, "zigzagged" through several people on his way to third base.

As he rounded third and headed home, Chambliss recalled, almost apologetically, "To get past one guy I knocked him down, ran him over, and raced into the dugout."

Then, at the urging of teammate Graig Nettles, Chambliss, accompanied by two policemen, returned to the home plate *area* so the umpires knew that he had touched the plate—or, at least, where the plate had been, before a fan tore it out of the ground.

On November 1, 1979, Chambliss was traded to Toronto, but 35 days later, before he ever wore a Blue Jays uniform, he was traded again, on December 5, to Atlanta. He played seven seasons for the Braves.

In 1985, while in Atlanta, Chambliss made $800,000, his peak salary. "I never reached a million dollars, but I have no regrets about my playing and coaching career," he said.

As for ongoing speculation about steroids in baseball, Chambliss said, "It's something that has been there but is just now coming out, and that's a shame. But bear in mind that baseball, *everybody* in baseball"—he said, obviously including the hierarchy of the game for emphasis—"loved Mark McGwire when he was hitting all those home runs [70, in 1998, and 65 in 1999]. It brought baseball back from the strike [of 1994] and, remember, McGwire was embraced for what he was able to do. Then came the stigma of steroids, and now they are calling it cheating."

Is it cheating? Chambliss was noncommittal.

"You have to understand that the idea of hitting a baseball is still a matter of making contact, good hand-eye coordination, and that a lot of talent is required. It's not just a matter of sheer strength," said the man who is highly regarded as a batting coach.

"Think of it this way. If you can hit a baseball that's going 95 miles an hour, steroids won't help you hit it better. Maybe farther, but you still have to make contact. Also, a guy who has bulked up [through the use of steroids] to help him hit the ball farther often is facing a pitcher who also has bulked up to help him throw the ball better. Or that he's cheating by throwing spitballs, or something like that."

Chambliss also talked about players today compared to those of his era. "It's sometimes difficult to get their respect," he said. "I'm lucky to have played and to have had a good career, so I can get through to most guys. It's not easy, but if you know what you're doing and make it clear what you want to do, it can work out OK. But if they [the players] are down on you and decide not to hear you . . . well, their contracts are guaranteed and nothing can make them listen if they don't want to listen."

Which is why Chambliss believes—as do others who know and respect him—that he deserves a chance to fulfill his ambition, to manage in the big leagues.

"I don't know if it will happen . . . I can only continue to hope," he said.

PAT
TABLER

First Baseman, Designated Hitter, Outfielder, Third Baseman, 1983–88

Best season: 1987, 151 games, .307 batting average, 11 home runs, 86 RBI

Indians career: 707 games, .294 avg., 39 home runs, 343 RBI

They called him "Mr. Clutch" when Pat Tabler played for the Indians, and it continued to be an appropriate nickname after he was traded to Kansas City in 1988, and later with the New York Mets and finally Toronto in 1992.

"I can't say I tried any harder when there were runners in scoring position because I like to think I tried hard all the time," said Tabler. "But I did have pretty good success driving in runs, especially when I played in Cleveland."

Which is putting it mildly.

In 1983, when he was acquired from the Chicago White Sox in one of the better deals made by Indian chiefs Gabe Paul and Phil Seghi—they traded shortstop Jerry Dybzinski to get him—Tabler hit .579 and drove in 25 runs in 19 bases-loaded situations.

In 1984 he batted .556 with 15 RBI in nine opportunities with runners in scoring position, and was even better in 1985 when his average was .857 with the bases loaded.

Overall, during his first five full seasons (1983–87) with the Tribe, prior to being traded to the Royals for pitcher Bud Black on June 3, 1988, Tabler went 29-for-55 for a .527 average.

"I can't explain it . . . it was just one of those things," said Tabler, who is now an analyst on television for Blue Jays games in Toronto, a job he says he loves almost as much as he did playing the game.

Tabler was born in Hamilton, Ohio, and raised in Cincinnati, where he still lives. He was an All-Ohio scholastic baseball and basketball player, and also ran track and played football at McNicholas High School. He and his wife, Susan, whom he married in 1979, have five children, including twin boys, Jake and Jaret, as well as sons Ty (Patrick Tyler), born 1982, and Troy, 1989, and daughter Kathryn, 1984.

Jake and Jaret were born in 1999—in Russia.

Tabler explained: "We had three children and my wife and I wanted more, but we couldn't. We decided we'd been blessed with everything we had, and that we wanted to have more kids and do something to help other children. So we went through an international adoption center. It was an eye-opening experience to go over there [to Russia], a life-changing experience to see how the conditions are in a country where the people have so little.

"I felt like God brought us together with these boys, who had a need just as Susan and I did. Their names were Boris and Roman, but I told Susan, 'They'll get their asses kicked on the playgrounds over here if they keep those names,' so we re-named them Jake and Jaret. They're both doing well and we're all very happy."

Tabler also is very happy in his broadcasting job, which began for him six months after his retirement as a player, following the Blue Jays victory in the 1992 World Series.

It was, as Tabler said, "kind of a coincidence" that got him into broadcasting—and also "something I'll always be grateful that happened."

Because he'd missed the 1993 Opening Day ceremonies when the Blue Jays presented the 1992 players with their World Series rings, Tabler was invited to spend a few days during the team's early season homestand.

"While I was there, one of the television broadcasters asked me

*"[Now] when the game is over I close my briefcase
and go home. I don't sit in the locker room and sulk
over going hitless and making a couple of errors."*

_____

to go on the air with him and talk about the team and what I was doing since I retired," said Tabler. "I spent a couple of innings on the air and, as luck would have it, one of the executives from TSN [The Sports Network] in Toronto was watching, contacted me and said, 'You'd be perfect for TSN [which was just getting started then].'"

TSN is the Canadian equivalent of the ESPN sports network.

"It turned out to be a good break. By the time I got home there was a phone message for me to go back to Toronto for an audition. I did, and I got the job." He's been in broadcasting ever since.

"It's a way for me to still be part of the game, which I always wanted to do, not as a manager but maybe as a coach," he said. "This way, when the game is over I close my briefcase and go home. I don't sit in the locker room and sulk over going hitless and making a couple of errors."

Which is not to say Tabler had a lot of those kind of days when he played for the Indians. In his five-plus seasons in Cleveland he had a cumulative batting average of .294 with 39 homers and 343 RBI in 707 games. His best batting average in Cleveland was in 1986, when he hit .326, fourth highest in the American League. He was a member of the A.L. all-star team in 1987. His major-league career average was .282 in 1,202 games over 12 seasons.

Tabler's highest salary, including bonuses, was $900,000 with the Blue Jays in 1992. The Indians paid him $800,000 in 1988, which pales in comparison to the money players are being paid today.

Tabler began as a first round (16th overall) choice of the New York Yankees in the 1976 amateur draft, but after six-plus seasons in the minor leagues he was traded in 1981 to the Chicago Cubs, who sent him to the White Sox in January 1983. He never played a regular season game for the White Sox and came to the Indians at the end of spring training that year.

"When I played in Cleveland, we didn't have the greatest of teams, but that didn't matter," he said. "We all felt we were building for something, working for something good that was going to happen. Unfortunately, it never did.

"We had a lot of good young players come through but we were always too young. We lost because we didn't know how to win. "But there were a lot of pleasant memories," continued Tabler. "Like the time we had won nine in a row on the road in 1986, and coming into Cleveland from Chicago there were news reports that a flash crowd would be at the Stadium that night—and there was. "We were playing Kansas City and forty- or fifty-thousand fans showed up.

"I came up in the ninth inning with the score tied, two outs, and the bases loaded, and I got a single off Dan Quisenberry to win the game. What a feeling it was. The crowd went wild, and I said, 'This is what it's going to be like if we ever get it together,' but we never did. Not while I was there, anyway."

Tabler did get a taste of winning in 1992 when the Blue Jays won the World Series. "There is nothing like winning the World Series, and knowing, when you walk off the field, that your team won the last game of the whole season and you are the world champs."

That's when he went home to Cincinnati and realized that it couldn't get any better. "I was 35, I'd played professionally for 17 years, my kids were getting older, and they and my wife needed me," he said.

"I had a chance to go to Japan for a million dollars, and I could have tried out with the Red Sox and the Phillies, but I didn't want to do that. I'd had enough.

"And I'm glad I did, especially considering all the good things that have happened to me since then."

ALAN
ASHBY

Catcher, 1973–76

Best season: 1976, 89 games,
.239 batting average, 4 home runs,
32 RBI

Indians career: 200 games,
.227 avg., 10 home runs, 67 RBI

Alan Ashby spent the better part of 17 major-league baseball seasons crouched behind the plate for some of the game's best pitchers. He caught a record-tying three no-hitters before he hung up his equipment in 1989.

But Ashby's career in baseball didn't end with his retirement as a player and, subsequently, a coach and minor-league manager. Switching from a baseball uniform to a business suit, Ashby went from behind the plate to behind a microphone as a radio voice of the Houston Astros from 1998 until 2006, when the Astros revamped their broadcasting crew. Ashby has also been doing freelance radio and television announcing in the Houston area.

While most of the highlights of his playing career occurred elsewhere, Ashby said he cherishes—admittedly with some reservations—his service with the Indians and often wonders about what might have been, back in the mid-1970s when financial problems constantly plagued the franchise.

"We had a group of good young players," he said, "Buddy Bell, Rick Manning, Duane Kuiper, George Hendrick, and Dennis Eckersley . . . to go with veterans like Frank Robinson, Gaylord Perry, and

Ray Fosse. I often wonder, if we'd been able to stay together and mature as a team, who knows how good we might have become?"

Ashby, selected in the third round of the 1969 amateur draft, made it to the Indians in 1973, was traded to Toronto in 1976, then played for Houston from 1979 to 1989. It was with the Astros that he established himself as an outstanding catcher.

"It'd be accurate to say that I had kind of a quiet career with the Indians," he mused. "Right after I came up with them, I know, I was a highly rated prospect. But then things kind of flipped around and . . . well, I wasn't so highly thought of by the regime running the club at that time. And to be honest, I wasn't too thrilled with the Cleveland organization either.

"It got better for me when Frank Robinson was hired [to manage in 1975] and I got a chance to play, to get my feet on the ground. One of my great memories was being there and seeing Frank hit a home run in his first game as manager of the Indians."

Ashby said he was "devastated" when the Tribe traded him on November 5, 1976, to Toronto. "I literally cried because I was leaving so many guys I came up with through the minors. I thought they wanted to keep me, and I wanted to stay with them."

It also was "disheartening" for Ashby the way he learned of the deal. "I got a call from a Toronto sportswriter before anybody with either the Indians or Blue Jays contacted me," he said.

He soon realized that getting away from the Indians "turned out to be good for me because I was able to develop as an everyday catcher, especially with the Astros. I got a chance to catch Nolan Ryan, and we won our division in 1980 and 1986."

It also was with the Astros that Ashby caught three no-hitters—by Ken Forsch in 1979, Ryan in 1981, and Mike Scott in 1986—and came close to catching two more. One, by Scott in 1988, was broken up with two out in the ninth; another by Ryan, also in 1988, ended with one out in the ninth.

Ashby's career-best season was 1987, when he batted .288 with 14 homers and 63 RBI for the Astros in 125 games.

Two years later, after playing his final major-league game for the Astros on May 9, 1989, they let him go. But he wasn't out of a job for long. Ashby became sports director of a Houston television station, managed in the minor leagues for three years (1994–96), and then served as the Astros bullpen coach in 1997.

The following season he went upstairs to the broadcast booth, launching a new career on radio. "I enjoyed playing, managing, and coaching, but I had a blast doing broadcasting," Ashby said before his contract with KTRH ended on December 20, 2005.

It was a lousy Christmas present for Ashby and his wife, Kathryn, whom he married in 1989. He and his first wife, Gayle, raised six children: daughters Kristin, Kelly, Kimberly, and Kara, and sons Jared and Justin.

"I was blind-sided . . . I never saw it coming," Ashby said of the decision by Astros owner Drayton McLane to not renew his contract. But I am determined to continue my [broadcasting] career, if not here [in Houston], then somewhere."

The only reason McLane gave for not renewing Ashby's contract was that the Astros were planning "to go in an entirely different direction."

"I've been told by some people that it's because I didn't wave pom-poms all the time," he said, meaning he wasn't a cheerleader.

Of Ashby's four seasons with the Indians, one of his most vivid memories is one that fans would prefer to forget: the infamous "Beer Night" riot on June 4, 1974, that caused the Tribe to forfeit a game to the Texas Rangers.

"I was the last official batter [in the top of the ninth inning] and singled," recalled Ashby. The Indians had just tied the score, 5-5, and Ashby was on first base and Rusty Torres on third with two out when trouble erupted.

"I can still see in my mind [Texas right fielder] Jeff Burroughs fighting off a guy who jumped out of the stands and crossed the foul line [in an attempt to grab Burroughs's cap]. It was bizarre . . . dangerous. Fights were breaking out everywhere."

"I often wonder, if we'd been able to stay together and mature as a team, who knows how good we might have become?"

Ashby's best contract with the Indians paid him $15,000 in 1975. That was a year before free agency came into being in major-league baseball. Twelve seasons later his salary climbed to a peak of $575,000.

He ended his playing career in 1989 with a .245 lifetime average in 1,370 games with 90 homers and 513 RBI. Shortly thereafter his broadcasting career began.

"To paraphrase an old cliché, all's well that ended well—for me," he said.

That, of course, was before Ashby's radio job in Houston ended.

In closing, Ashby also was surprisingly candid in his comments regarding the state of the game, especially concerning the wild escalation of player salaries that has taken place the last several years.

"I hate to see the way the Yankees' payroll has gone over $200 million," he said. "They have the kind of revenue that allows it and an owner who will spend whatever he thinks it will take to buy a championship. But it's unfair. It's a crying shame. I really believe that, when the owners and players had their last major confrontation [in negotiations for a Collective Bargaining Agreement in 2002], if the owners had stuck to their guns they could have won.

"And if they had, it would have put themselves in the position of saying, 'OK, boys, here are the new ground rules. We are going to have not only a salary cap, but also a salary floor.' It would have forced teams to compete, and if there were any unable to compete [financially], they would have had to get out of the game. It would have created true competitive balance, which I think would be the best thing for the game and the fans.

"It's really amazing that owners of a business like this can't say, 'Hey, guys, let's do this to solve our problems.' But if they collectively do that, they're in trouble because they'd be accused of collusion."

And now, though Ashby no longer plays baseball, it's obvious that he talks the game very well—and expects to continue doing so.

TOM
CANDIOTTI

Pitcher, 1986–91, 1999

Best season: 1986, 36 games,
16-12 won-lost record, 0 saves,
3.57 ERA

Indians career: 183 games,
73-66 won-lost record, 0 saves,
3.67 ERA

Tom Candiotti reluctantly hung up his spikes in 1999 after pitching 2,725 innings in 451 games during a 16-year major-league career with the Indians and four other teams.

But he's still throwing strikes—even a perfect game.

Except that the strikes Candiotti throws now are in tournaments sponsored by the Professional Bowling Association, and his "perfecto" was a 300 game in 2004. He also has rolled a couple of 299s, which could be considered one-hitters in baseball (of which he threw two for the Tribe in 1987, one against New York spoiled by an eighth-inning single by Mike Easler).

The former knuckleball pitcher—who prefers to be called "a pitcher who threw knuckleballs"—compiled a major-league won-lost record of 151-164 with the Indians, Milwaukee Brewers, Toronto, Los Angeles, and Oakland. In six-plus seasons in Cleveland, he was 73-66.

Candiotti's preference for being called "a pitcher who threw knuckleballs" is because he was a fastball-curveball pitcher—though not very successful—early in his professional baseball career that began in the Class A Northwest League in 1979. It wasn't until he started "messing around" with a knuckleball in spring training with Milwaukee in 1985, after two so-so seasons with the Brewers, that Candiotti was encouraged to work on the pitch.

He went back to the minors in 1985 to perfect his knuckleball, which he says got him to the major leagues with the Indians, though he continued to throw his other pitches, albeit not as often.

Candiotti also had to overcome a serious injury to his right elbow in order to continue his professional baseball career. In October 1981, after he'd been selected by the Brewers in the minor-league draft, he underwent "Tommy John surgery." At that time the operation had been performed previously on only eight pitchers, just one of whom—Tommy John himself—was able to resume his career.

Candiotti missed all of 1982, but the operation obviously was successful. He was up and down between Milwaukee and the minor leagues from 1983 to 1985, after which he became a free agent and signed with the Indians. He later pitched for the Blue Jays, Dodgers, and Athletics—and the Indians again in 1999—before he retired from baseball with two bad knees at the age of 42. He pitched his final game on July 24, 1999.

Now, in addition to his new career as a professional bowler, Candiotti also competes for what he calls "profitable purses" in golf on the Celebrity Players Tour—but only when he's not on the air for ESPN and Toronto Blue Jays telecasts.

He also appeared in the movie *61**, chronicling the 1961 season of Mickey Mantle and Roger Maris. Candiotti played the role of Hoyt Wilhelm.

Candiotti does color commentary on ESPN for the Little League World Series and "a handful" of major-league games, and "thirty or so" Blue Jays games when they play in Seattle, Anaheim, Oakland, and Texas.

"I probably could do more [in broadcasting] but I don't like to travel too far east" from Scottsdale, Arizona, where he makes his home with wife Donna and their two sons, Casey and Clark.

"I enjoy broadcasting, but it's bowling and golf that really turn me on now," said Candiotti. "Once you're finished in baseball, when they pull the plug on you, it's hard to turn off the competitive juices."

In addition to earning his BPA card, Candiotti also is a "near scratch" golfer and regularly is invited to play in celebrity tournaments.

Candiotti was the Indians' winningest pitcher (16-12) in 1986 when he led the American League with 17 complete games. He also was the leading winner (15 victories) on the 1990 staff, but his first tour of duty in Cleveland ended five years later—unhappily for him—on June 27, 1991, when he was traded to Toronto. "I felt, basically, that I was run out of town," he said.

It came in the wake of what he called "a contract problem" the previous winter when his agent negotiated a $2.5 million salary, which was a huge raise over the $1.05 million he was paid in 1990 when his record was 15-11.

"I was broken up when the Indians traded me," Candiotti said. "I was raised in California, but it was in Cleveland that I grew up as a pitcher, where I was successful and felt comfortable. I loved everything about it and felt we were making progress as a team.

"I gave everything I had to the organization, and then they got rid of me. John Hart had just come in as general manager and [the Indians] probably wanted to get some young guys in there who could gel at the same time, which is what happened.

"My contract probably had something to do with it, but I think they were just giving up on 1991 and 1992, and getting ready to have a contending club by 1994 when they moved into their new ballpark.

"But, as it turned out, being traded was a good opportunity for me. I went from a team that would lose over 100 games to a pennant contender in Toronto where there were 50,000 fans for every game, and got into the playoffs."

In 1991, his record was 7-6 with the Indians and 6-7 with the Blue Jays, after which Candiotti became a free agent again and signed a

> *"I was going on 42, and before every game the*
> *trainer drained fluid from my knees, then injected*
> *them . . . it was like changing the oil in your car.*

four-year, $15.5 million contract with the Dodgers. In December 1995 he re-signed with them for $6 million through 1997. In his six seasons in L.A., Candiotti's won-lost record was 52-64.

Candiotti's next stop was Oakland, with a two-year contract worth $5.85 million, but after posting an 11-16 mark in 1998, he didn't survive the second season. With a 3-5 record, two bad knees, and the A's having several young pitching prospects waiting in the wings, Candiotti was released on June 16, 1999.

"By then I was going on 42, and before every game the trainer drained fluid from my knees, then injected them . . . it was almost like changing the oil in your car. Trying to compete was no longer fun."

But when the Indians called two weeks later, Candiotti's competitive juices started flowing again, and he welcomed the chance to return to Cleveland.

"When Hart said the Indians were looking for some help—he called it 'looking for another arm to add to our pitching arsenal'—I couldn't say no to the opportunity."

But it lasted only five weeks. On August 2, after appearing in seven games with one victory and one loss, Candiotti's knee trouble surfaced again. An MRI showed that he had torn cartilage in his left knee, and that "all kinds of garbage" was floating around in his right knee. He was released and went home.

That still wasn't the end, however. After a third knee operation, Candiotti said, "By January [2000] I was feeling pretty good," and called former teammate Bud Black, the pitching coach for the Los Angeles Angels. "The competitive juices were flowing again," Candiotti admitted.

The Angels welcomed him back, but it was no use. The same old pain returned, and Candiotti finally quit during spring training. "It's hard to kill a knuckleballer, but by then I was satisfied I couldn't do it anymore. I didn't leave anything on the table," he said.

"I have no regrets, and if I had my career to do all over again, the only thing I'd change—or that I'd *want* to change—was being traded by Cleveland. That was the low point of my career."

And the high point? "Well, just let me say that one of my biggest thrills was to see my name on the [2005] Hall of Fame ballot—and then getting a couple of votes. I had no expectation of making it, but it was great that two writers voted for me."

CHARLIE
SPIKES

Outfielder, Designated Hitter
1973–77

Best season: 1974, 155 games,
.271 batting average, 22 home runs,
80 RBI

Indians career: 539 games,
.246 avg., 62 home runs, 228 RBI

He was immediately dubbed the "Bogalusa Bomber," more in anticipation of what was expected from him than what he previously had delivered. And, unfortunately, as it turned out, the nickname didn't hold up for Charlie Spikes, who'd been the biggest celebrity ever to come out of Bogalusa, Louisiana.

Oh, initially Spikes showed signs of being something very special. He arrived in Cleveland in the first of several deals that raised eyebrows among the cynics who wondered if maybe—just *maybe*— too close a bond still existed between Phil Seghi and Gabe Paul.

Paul, who'd been the chief executive of the Indians from 1961 to 1972 and Seghi's longtime friend, boss, and mentor, left Cleveland at the end of the 1972 season to take over as president of the New York Yankees under owner George Steinbrenner. Seghi replaced Paul as general manager and, less than two months later, on November 27, 1972, the Indians (*read*: Seghi) traded all-star third baseman Graig Nettles and catcher Gerry Moses to the Yankees (*read*: Paul) for Spikes and three journeymen players—catcher John Ellis, infielder Jerry Kenney, and outfielder Rusty Torres.

Spikes, who at age 18 had been a first round (11th overall) selection of the Yankees in the 1969 amateur draft and received a $38,000 signing bonus, put together three outstanding minor league seasons (1970–72). He was especially good in 1972 when he hammered 26 homers and hit .309 in the Class AA Eastern League. Which, of course, created great interest among several clubs, including the Indians, who—as usual in that era—were struggling on the field and at the gate.

Hence the deal with the Yankees between Seghi and Paul that brought the Bogalusa Bomber to Cleveland.

Spikes's first two years with the Indians were promising. He led the team in home runs and RBI, with 23 and 73 in 1973, and 22 and 80 in 1974.

"That was the real Charlie Spikes, who was just getting started but then never really got going," he said from his home in Bogalusa. "I wish I could go back and do it over again."

Surely, the Indians do, too.

Three decades later, Spikes himself isn't sure what happened. Or why. His production went into rapid decline the next three seasons, through 1977, while his strikeouts increased equally rapidly, to an average of one every 5.7 times at-bat.

On December 9, 1977, Spikes was traded to Detroit, where he played briefly for the Tigers and in their minor-league system in 1978 without improvement, then in Atlanta for two seasons (1979–80). Finally, he wound up in Japan in 1981, until a severe knee injury ended his career midway through the season.

Some blamed Spikes's downfall on Frank Robinson, who came to the Indians as player-manager in 1975. In the *Baseball Almanac,* published on the Internet, it is written: "Frank Robinson made [Spikes] a special project . . . but Spikes skidded under Robinson's often caustic criticism."

But Spikes doesn't blame Robinson.

"I guess a big part of my problem in the beginning was that I was too immature. Maybe it would have been different, better for me, if I had spent more time in the minor leagues, or if I had not been so young when the Yankees drafted me," said Spikes. "It also might have been that things came too easy for me when I was in the minor leagues, before I found out how much tougher it was in the big leagues.

"But it wasn't Frank," he said again. "I liked playing for him, and I wanted to do good for him because he was baseball's first black manager. If anything, maybe I tried too hard. But if I did, that was my fault, not his."

Spikes's only criticism, albeit implied, of Robinson was that, "I think he thought everybody should be able to do as good as he did, but everybody can't."

It's also probable that injuries were a major factor in Spikes's fall from grace. Especially one he suffered in Puerto Rico during the winter season of 1974–75. He was hit in the face with a pitch that closed his left eye for more than two weeks. It probably affected his vision, though subsequent examinations indicated there was no permanent damage.

"I didn't realize it at the time, but I don't think I could see as good afterwards. If anything, I might have come back too soon," he said.

Whether his eyesight was impaired or, perhaps, the injury caused him to become "gun-shy" at the plate, nobody really knows, especially Spikes. But the fact is, early in the following season Spikes went 0-for-21 and was benched.

"Frank took me out of the lineup, and when I got back in, if I didn't hit good, he took me out again. I could never get really comfortable, but that was the only problem we ever had that I can remember," he said.

Neither would Spikes confirm that perhaps he became apprehensive after being hit in the face with a pitch a few months earlier. "Not that I know," he said. "I was never scared when I went to the plate."

After his brief trial in 1978 with the Tigers and their Class AAA farm club in Evansville, Indiana, Spikes was released.

"I figured my career was over," he said, "but then I got a call from

"I did OK in Japan, but it was tough to stay focused. I had trouble communicating, and the fans are so excitable, like football fans."

Bobby Cox," who had been Spikes's manager in 1972 in the Eastern League. "He remembered me and invited me to try out with Atlanta," the National League team Cox then managed.

Spikes jumped at the chance and won a job, though it was only as a pinch hitter and part-time player. He batted .280 in 66 games in 1979, and .278 in 41 games the following season. But when it ended, so did Spikes's major-league career at the age of 29. The Braves released him.

"I didn't blame them. I was getting old, my knees were bothering me, and they had a lot of young players coming up," said Spikes. But he still didn't quit.

The Chunichi Dragons in Japan offered him a $236,000 contract—U.S. dollars, the most money Spikes ever made—and he accepted. It was more than five times as much as the $44,000 the Indians paid him in 1976, though his peak salary in the major leagues climbed to $65,000, which he received from the Braves in 1979.

"I did OK in Japan. I think I hit 12 or 13 home runs, but it was tough to stay focused. I had trouble communicating, and the fans are so different over there," he said. "They're very excitable, like football fans are in this country."

An even larger problem for Spikes was that he re-injured a knee midway through the season. "That's when I knew it was over," he said. "I needed an operation and came home," which finally did end the baseball career of the one-time Bogalusa Bomber.

It was while he worked in a textile factory in 1989 that Spikes hurt his back. "I was lifting a box and something popped," he said. "I couldn't straighten up." It was a ruptured disk. Another back operation followed. His third. Also surgery on his knee.

"Those are the only regrets I have about my career," he said, referring to his injuries. "But I have no complaints. I'm grateful for the opportunity I had to play that game. I just wish I could have been better, for longer."

Now on total disability, Spikes is back in Bogalusa with his wife Marsha, whom he married in 1972, and their two daughters, Kimberly Charmaine, who was born in 1977, and Leslie Anastasia, born in 1981.

"I have a fine wife and two fine daughters, and I am a happy man," he said.

"I was a celebrity when I first signed with the Yankees, but not anymore, although I still get requests in the mail for my autograph. Not a lot, but some, and it's kind of nice.

"It's like, when you guys started calling me the 'Bogalusa Bomber.' At first it was kind of embarrassing. But then I got used to it and I liked it. Actually, I enjoyed every minute of it.

"But nobody calls me that anymore. Not until you just did."

JERRY
KINDALL

Second Base, Shortstop, First Base,
1962–64

Best season: 1962, 154 games,
.232 batting average, 13 home runs,
55 RBI

Indians career: 263 games,
.228 avg., 20 home runs, 77 RBI

He was known as a "glove man" during his nine-season major-league playing career, a defensive specialist who *saved* his team more runs than he produced. And, as such, Jerry Kindall, who never batted .300 or hit many home runs, seldom got his name in headlines on the sports pages, nor did he get the credit he deserved.

Not, that is, until he retired as a player and became one of the nation's most successful college coaches, earning recognition as an outstanding baseball technician.

Oh, there was one weekend back in 1962, June 15-17, when Kindall was the talk of Cleveland as he led the Indians—with his bat—to a four-game sweep of the hated New York Yankees. He got eight hits, including two home runs, in his first nine trips to the plate.

He called it one of the two highlights of his playing career, which began with the Chicago Cubs in 1956, continued with the Indians from 1962 to 1964, and ended with Minnesota in 1965.

"The other was in 1960, with the Cubs, when I made a couple of good plays to preserve Don Cardwell's no-hitter against St. Louis," said the former second baseman. "It was the second game of a double header in Wrigley Field. I don't think I got a hit in that game . . . and if I did, I don't remember. But I do remember the plays I made."

Spoken like a true Glove Man.

"I loved my career, except that I would've liked to have played longer," he said. "But Calvin Griffith [the owner of the Twins] thought otherwise."

Griffith released Kindall after he played 125 games in 1965. Though he batted only .196 with six home runs, he fielded almost every ball that was hit near him as the Twins were winning the American League pennant.

Kindall, who'd been an All-American shortstop for the University of Minnesota which won the national championship in 1956, signed with the Cubs when he was 21. They paid him $50,000 over three years, including salary and bonuses, and because of a rule then in effect, Kindall spent most of the next two seasons on the Cubs' bench, playing behind—or, as he said, "spelling"—future Hall of Famer Ernie Banks. The rule required that an amateur free agent who was paid $4,000 or more to sign—as Kindall was—had to be kept on the team's major league-roster for two seasons.

After Kindall served his penance, he was switched to second base and sent to the minor leagues for the next three seasons (1958–60). He was called back by the Cubs in 1960, traded to the Indians in 1961, and then dealt to the Twins in 1964.

Upon his release by the Twins, Kindall began what he calls the "second half of my baseball life," which gave him great satisfaction and earned him much more credit.

Kindall, who grew up in St. Paul, Minnesota, returned to the University of Minnesota as an assistant basketball coach in 1966. Two years later he also became an assistant to baseball coach Dick Siebert, a former major-league first baseman.

When Frank Sancet retired in 1972 as the highly successful baseball coach at the University of Arizona, Kindall applied and got the job. It launched a head-coaching career that resulted in accolades, honors, and championships over the next 24 years.

Kindall's team won the NCAA (College) World Series in 1976 and again won the national championship in 1980 and 1986, after losing in the finals in 1979 and 1985. After each of those winning seasons, Kindall was named the college baseball Coach of the Year. Numerous other honors were bestowed on Kindall in subsequent seasons, prior to his retirement on August 1, 1996, as the winningest coach in the history of the University of Arizona with a record of 860-580-6.

Equally satisfying to Kindall is that more than 200 former players at Arizona went on to play professional baseball. Thirty-two reached the major leagues, including four with the Indians: catcher Ron Hassey, first baseman (and later Boston manager) Terry Francona, outfielder Kenny Lofton, and infielder Tommy Hinzo.

"I've been asked if there's a former player of mine who stands out over the rest," said Kindall. "I'd have to name three—Hassey, Francona, and an outfielder named Dave Stegman, who played for the Tigers, Yankees, and White Sox [from 1978 to 1984]."

Kindall called Hassey, at that time the bench coach for Seattle, "one of our leaders the year we won in 1976, and one of the great competitors I've coached."

Speaking of Francona, Kindall said, "His father [Tito] and I were teammates in Cleveland. When Terry was in high school, Tito called me and said Terry was quite a player, a better player than he was. Tito wanted him to go to Arizona."

Another highlight for Kindall—actually, what he called "the highest honor I have received in my baseball life"—took place on January 24, 2004. That's when the University of Arizona recognized Kindall and Frank Sancet, his predecessor as the Wildcats coach, by re-dedicating the college's baseball facility as "Jerry Kindall Field at Frank Sancet Stadium."

Kindall called his dual careers in baseball "a wonderful combination," especially the nearly quarter of a century he coached at Arizona.

"It has meant the most because I always wanted to be a coach—

*"All the guys, my teammates with every team
I played for, knew where I stood, as far as my
faith was concerned, and they respected me."*

---

actually, a coach-teacher—and got the chance to do so at two great universities, Arizona and Minnesota."

Of the first half of his baseball life, Kindall admitted, "I was disappointed when the Cubs traded me to Cleveland because I had been a Cubbie for six years and a fan of theirs for a long time. I loved them. But Mr. [Gabe] Paul gave me a good raise and [manager] Mel McGaha played me every day. That made [1962] my most enjoyable year as a player. I have a very fond place in my heart for Cleveland."

Kindall and his second wife, Diane, whom he married in 1988, make their home in Tucson, Arizona. His first wife, Georgia, died in 1987 of Amyotrophic Lateral Sclerosis, better known as Lou Gehrig's Disease. They were married nearly 31 years and had four children: Becky, Doug, Bruce, and Martha. Diane also was widowed in 1987.

Kindall said he never "in my saner moments" aspired to manage or coach in the big leagues, although he admitted, "It always lingered in the back of my mind that I could do something worthwhile in professional baseball."

A devout Christian who diligently practices his faith, Kindall said there were times he was troubled by some of the things he saw happening in professional baseball.

"But all the guys, my teammates with every team I played for, knew where I stood, as far as my faith was concerned, and they respected me. I was never hassled because of my faith, and I always knew the places where I was going, and I chose the guys I wanted to go with."

Since his retirement from the "second half" of his baseball life,

Kindall has written and edited several books on baseball, including *The Science of Coaching* and *Sports Illustrated Baseball*. He also has produced numerous pamphlets on baseball.

"After all the years I coached, there are times I miss it, though I still do some with USA Baseball and Major League Baseball International."

He travels extensively as a director and member of the executive committee of USA Baseball, broadcasts college games for the NCAA and several college conferences, and, of course, remains very active with and totally dedicated to the Fellowship of Christian Athletes.

"I also go to Europe in the summer to coach under Major League Baseball International," he said. "In 2001 and 2002, I worked with baseball people in Sweden, and in the summer of 2004, I was in southern France for five weeks teaching and coaching.

"I thoroughly love what I am doing . . . which is not to say I have no regrets about my life in baseball. I do. My first life, if you will. I wish I had done better those early years with the Cubbies and the Indians.

"But I also believe I found my niche. That, for me, coaching the game was better than playing the game," he said. "For me."

JOE
LIS

—

Outfielder, 1974–76

Best season: 1976, 20 games,
.314 batting average, 2 home runs,
7 RBI

Indians career: 86 games,
.243 avg., 10 home runs, 31 RBI

Joe Lis played eight years in the major leagues but was never a regular. In fact, only once did he appear in as many as 100 games in a season while compiling a career batting average of .233 with four teams.

But that doesn't mean he didn't *know how* to hit, as Lis said from his home in Evansville, Indiana, where, since 1999, he has operated the Joe Lis Baseball School, Inc.

"I teach kids what the good hitters taught me, the things that Rico Carty and Harmon Killebrew taught me, or tried to teach me, when I was playing," he said.

"I don't mind telling you I am the best batting coach there is. I watch more than a million swings every year in my school, and I'll go up against anybody, any coach.

"One of the reasons the kids like my school is because I know what it's like to be six years old."

Then, "Actually, I'm a senior citizen going on 22," he said.

"I tell the kids, I didn't play much, but I always played hard, and most of the time I had fun. I know what it's like to make mistakes because I've made lots of them. I've been booed by 55,000 fans in a ballpark, and I've screwed up in front of 55 million more on television. But you can't let it get you down. You have to keep trying hard."

Lis said there usually are about 140 to 150 boys in his school, ranging in age from six to eighteen, with "seventy-five or so" on a waiting list to get in.

One of his students is a nephew of Don Mattingly, who won the American League batting championship in 1984 and retired with a .307 career average. "The [Mattingly] kid has been coming to my school for the last six or seven years . . . how about that for an endorsement?" he wanted to know.

"I'd like to get back into [professional] baseball, but when you do, you have to divorce your wife, and I don't want to divorce Susan. We went to high school together [in Somerville, New Jersey] and got married in 1966." That was two years after Lis was signed at age 17 as an amateur free agent by Philadelphia.

"The Phillies gave me a $15,000 signing bonus, which was pretty good money in those days, and that should tell you what kind of a prospect I was."

Lis toiled seven years in the minors, played for the Phillies from 1970 to 1972, spent 1973 and part of 1974 with Minnesota, and was sold to the Indians on June 5, 1974. In his first game for the Tribe, Lis hit a home run to help Gaylord Perry beat Kansas City.

"After the game Gaylord gave me 25 bucks, which he did for everybody who hit a home run for him," said Lis. "But if you did something bad when he was pitching, you didn't have to pay him back, but the grief he gave you was even worse."

When he played for the Indians, Lis said, "Somebody in the front office, either [general manager] Phil Seghi or [owner] Ted Bonda came up with the bright idea to hire a psychologist—we called him 'Dale Carnegie'—to motivate us.

"We'd meet with the guy once a week when we were on the road, and everybody would go except for George Hendrick, which was crazy because he was the main reason they hired the guy. But, like they say in Boston about Manny Ramirez, that 'Manny is Manny,' George was going to be George, no matter what.

"I enjoyed the [parts of] three seasons I played for Cleveland, probably because I didn't play enough for anybody to say bad things about me."

Lis's highest salary in baseball was $36,000 in 1977, when he played for Seattle, his last season in the major leagues. He retired two years later after batting .292 with 16 homers and 80 RBI for Class AAA Evansville, then Detroit's top farm club. "When the Tigers didn't put me on their roster, I got the message. It was time to quit."

Joe and Susan raised three children: daughter Becky, who is an outstanding fast-pitch softball player, and sons Jimmy and Joey. The latter played in the minor leagues for the Indians and Toronto, and now works with his dad in the baseball school.

"Life is good," said Lis. "I had triple bypass heart surgery a few years ago, and I feel great."

Though Lis never was a star, he was well liked by the media, one of the reasons being that he was never at a loss for words—and still isn't—though he didn't always choose them carefully. A case in point: Lis certainly didn't endear himself to Frank Robinson the day in mid-September 1974 that Robinson joined the Indians. Three weeks later Robinson would become player-manager.

Lis was seated in front of his locker—and between the lockers of Perry and Robinson—when Robinson arrived as the "right-handed bat" Seghi said the Tribe needed "to make a run for the pennant." Within a matter of minutes Perry and Robinson got into a heated argument. Robinson was angered by an item in the paper quoting Perry saying that he wanted "a dollar more" in salary than Robinson was demanding. A fight almost ensued.

It didn't, probably because of Lis, who said of the incident, "I told Frank, 'Don't we have enough problems without more of this crap?' and I said to both of them, 'Why don't you two guys either get it on [fight], or get the hell out of the clubhouse." That calmed

"I tell the kids, I didn't play much,
but I always played hard,
and most of the time I had fun."

———————————————

the confrontation, but it didn't end the antagonism between Perry and Robinson. The following season Perry was traded to Texas.

It also was Lis's opinion that his intervention in the quarrel between the two men, and his reprimand of Robinson, damaged his relationship with the new manager.

"We were never the same after that," said Lis, and the record bears him out. He spent most of the next two seasons in the minors after being demoted by Robinson.

Lis also had words—and, subsequently, problems—with Seghi in 1976. The Indians promoted a rookie instead of Lis to fill a vacancy on the roster created by an injury to Boog Powell. At the time, Lis said, he was batting "something like .360 with 16 homers" at Class AAA Toledo,

"I told Phil, 'I'm in Toledo busting my ass and hitting the hell out of the ball, and you call up a kid who has one home run. What the hell is going on?'" said Lis. "Phil screamed at me, 'Who are you to tell me what to do,' and a lot of crap like that.

"Finally, they called me up in September and I got more hits [16-for-51, .314] that month than Robinson got the entire year [15-for-67, .224]. So, no, I was never very happy with Robinson or Seghi," said Lis—and it's safe to assume they were not very happy with him. When the season ended, the Indians made Lis available in the expansion draft of 1976, and he was claimed by Seattle.

He played for the Mariners—though not much and not very well—in 1977, went to Japan in 1978, and returned for one final attempt to make it back to the major leagues with Detroit. But after two seasons in the minors, he retired and went back to school—the Joe Lis Baseball School, Inc.

BROOK
JACOBY

Third Baseman, 1984–91, 1992

Best season: 1987, 155 games, .300 batting average, 32 home runs, 69 RBI

Indians career: 1,240 games, .273 avg., 120 home runs, 524 RBI

In Atlanta, back in 1983 when the Braves were in a tight race for the National League West championship and a berth in the World Series, the fans were—initially—ecstatic to learn that Len Barker, he of perfect-game fame, would be coming to their team's aid.

And in Cleveland, at that time, fans of the Indians were angry when they learned their team was dumping off another high-priced player for three nobodies and, as usual in those days, a large sum of money. It all revolved around the August 28, 1983, trade that sent Barker to the Braves for three players to be named later and $150,000. But soon thereafter the emotions of fans in both cities changed 180 degrees.

The truth be told, it became one of the few times, in those pre-Jacobs Field era—a.k.a. the "bad old days" in Tribe annals—that the front-office tandem of Gabe Paul and Phil Seghi got the clear-cut best of a rival general manager.

It turned out that way after the October 21, 1983, delivery of Brook Jacoby and center fielder Brett Butler, two of the three players to be named in the deal for Barker. Seven weeks earlier the Indians received rookie pitcher Rick Behenna.

At the time Barker, who had been considered the ace of the

Cleveland pitching staff and, as such, was one of the team's highest paid players, had an 8-13 record. After going to Atlanta, Barker, obviously on the downside of his otherwise splendid career, won only one game while losing three for the Braves in the final month of the 1983 season. He compiled a final 10-20 record through the next two seasons and was released in 1985.

At the same time that Atlanta fans were becoming disillusioned with Barker, Tribe fans began exulting in the play of Jacoby and Butler, though Behenna, a seldom-used reliever, never won a game and lost seven before he was released in 1985.

Jacoby, a rookie when he came to Cleveland, and Butler, with only one full major-league season on his resume, became key players for the Indians; Jacoby for eight-plus seasons and Butler for four.

As happy as were the Cleveland fans, Jacoby was even happier.

"I was stuck behind [Braves star third baseman] Bob Horner and had no place to go in Atlanta," said Jacoby, whose father, Brook Sr., was a minor-league pitcher in the Indians and Philadelphia Phillies organizations three decades earlier.

Jacoby and his wife, Pam, whom he married in 1982, have three children: sons Brook III and Torrey, born in 1986 and 1988, respectively, and daughter Sierra in 1995.

A seventh-round selection of the Braves in the amateur draft of 1979, Jacoby received two brief trials with the Braves—11 games in 1981 (going 2-for-10), and four games in 1983 (0-for-8).

It was different, however, upon his coming to Cleveland, where it was a rapid rise to distinction. Jacoby launched his Tribe career in 1984 and soon was recognized as a sure-handed, solid third baseman and dependable hitter with above-average power.

He was an American League all-star in 1986 and 1990, and was elected the Indians Man of the Year in 1987 when he batted .300 with 32 homers and 69 RBI.

It also was in 1987, on July 3 against Chicago, that Jacoby became one of only 12 players in Tribe history to hit three consecutive home runs in one game.

Upon his retirement in 1992, Jacoby coached briefly at Ventura

Junior College. He left, he said, "Because the intensity and work ethic [of the players] wasn't really what I thought it should have been . . . when I realized the kids couldn't wait to get off the field and go do whatever they were doing."

Jacoby played part of a season in Japan in 1993, "But I lasted only about three months because I didn't feel I could get on the field everyday and play the way I wanted, the way I should. I wasn't happy with myself."

He subsequently coached for Atlantic City in an independent professional league, in the minors for Cincinnati for three years through 2002, and joined Texas as its minor-league roving hitting coordinator through 2005. In 2006 he was the interim batting coach for the Rangers.

Of his career with the Indians, Jacoby said, "I loved it. The only thing that would have made it better would have been if we'd had a better team, if we'd done better."

The Indians did have—or, at least, *appeared* to have—the makings of a very good team in 1986. Not only did the "experts" believe it, so did the fans.

In Jacoby's opinion, it was the fans' unbridled enthusiasm, especially in late April and early May of 1986, that played a major role in keeping the franchise in Cleveland when speculation was rampant that it would be relocated because of failing attendance.

"We had a 10-game winning streak [from April 26–May 7], which probably was the first time something like that had happened in Cleveland in quite awhile. We were tied for first place with New York in the A.L. East [with a 17-8 record] and the fans were really excited," he said. "We came off the road and the Stadium was packed. It was outstanding to see all those people come to see us and cheer for us.

"To me—obviously to a lot of us—it proved that if you put a competitive team on the field, the fans will come out.

"I like to think that what we did back then helped make it possible for what's happening in Cleveland now. That was such a pivotal time, whether there was going to continue to be a team playing in Cleveland or not."

Although the 1986 Indians fell out of contention in August and finished with an 84-78 record, their attendance soared to 1,471,977, the highest in 27 years, and second most since 1951, raising everybody's expectations for the following season.

Even *Sports Illustrated*, for its April 6, 1987 issue, pictured two Tribe players—Cory Snyder and Joe Carter—on the cover with the headline, "Indian Uprising," and the prediction, "Believe it, Cleveland is the best team in the American League."

"We were all kind of surprised, and at the end [of the season] it was very embarrassing. If it hadn't been so disappointing, it would have been funny," Jacoby said.

In 1987, before he was fired as manager, Pat Corrales spoke of his high regard for the soft-spoken, unassuming Jacoby.

"There is no one on this club who is more respected for his work habits and the example he sets for others," Corrales said then. "What you will see is Brook Jacoby at the ballpark early and often working. What you won't see is a sulking, face-to-the-locker bad apple if he happened to have a bad game."

Not only did the Indians fail to live up to *Sports Illustrated's* great expectations in 1987, they became only the fourth team in franchise history to lose more than 100 games.

They were never higher than fifth in the 1987 standings and spent all but the first five games in seventh [and last] place, finishing with an abysmal 61-101 record.

"We had some good young players that year [namely Jacoby himself, Butler, Carter, Julio Franco, Snyder and Pat Tabler], but we didn't have the pitching," said Jacoby. "Rick Sutcliffe and Bert Blyleven had been traded to get the nucleus of some young hitters, and when you look at what they did after they left Cleveland . . . well, they went on to have very good careers."

And so began, the following winter, another of many previous and subsequent rebuilding projects by the Indians.

Jacoby remained a staple of the team until he was traded to Oakland on July 26, 1991, as he would have become a free agent at the end of the season. He re-signed with the Indians in 1992, hit .261 in 120 games, and retired with a career batting average of .270 with 120 homers and 545 RBI.

Two years later the franchise would move into a new home and embark upon a true resurgence on the field and at the gate, as Jacoby had foretold with such certainty a decade earlier.

KEN
ASPROMONTE

Second Baseman/Third Baseman,
1960–62 (Manager, 1972–74)

Best season: 1960, 117 games,
.290 batting average, 10 home runs,
48 RBI

Indians career: 159 games,
.275 avg., 10 home runs, 54 RBI

By Ken Aspromonte's own admission, "I realized too late that my temper hurt me throughout my baseball career," which ended in 1974 when he was replaced by Frank Robinson, who became the first African American manager in major-league baseball.

And while Aspromonte was, at the very least, an average offensive and defensive player—he won the batting championship of the Pacific Coast League in 1957—he further conceded that his too-fiery disposition often was a factor in his being dealt from one team to another during his nomadic seven-season career.

Aspromonte played for six major-league teams—beginning in 1957 with Boston (which signed him as an amateur free agent in 1950), Washington, the Indians, Los Angeles Angels, and Milwaukee Braves, and finishing with the Chicago Cubs in 1963—but never stayed with any team more than two years.

The Indians traded with the Washington Senators to get him on May 15, 1960, lost him nine months later to the Angels in the American League expansion draft, re-acquired him in a waiver deal on July 3, 1961, then traded him to the Braves on June 24, 1962.

Now semi-retired after he and his brother Bob, also a former major leaguer, owned a lucrative Coors beer distributorship in Houston for nearly thirty years, Aspromonte offered this self-appraisal of his ability as a player.

"I think I was pretty good. No, I *know* I was pretty good. Not great, but good. I had very good statistics in the minor leagues, but once I got to the major leagues I started fighting myself, primarily because I was never satisfied. I always wanted to be better.

"I also hate to admit that I was one of those guys who could not shake off a bad situation. I analyzed myself to death, wondering what the hell I did that was wrong. Why I didn't stick with any one organization. It really got to me. Looking back at it, I don't think anybody was ever patient enough with me, at least not in my opinion.

"Hey, I grew up in Brooklyn—Bensonhurst, New York—not Westchester County, in a neighborhood of tough kids where you had to fight your way through everything if you wanted to get to the top. Most of my friends were fighters, and I was one of them. But eventually I found out you don't fight in professional sports. All you can do is try the best you can with whatever God-given ability you have and hope it's good enough.

"If there was any time in my life I needed someone to talk to, it was then, when I was in the big leagues. But in those days they didn't have guys like that, guys who could sit down with you and talk to you and help you. They just threw you out there, and if you produced, fine. And if you didn't produce, there were plenty of other players out there waiting for their chance.

"I got better control of myself after I went into managing."

He first managed in the minor leagues for the Indians in 1968, two years after he retired following three seasons (1964–66) in the Japanese Central League playing for the Taiyo Whales.

"Unfortunately, I didn't realize until it was too late that it was my temper, my disposition that kept me from being the player I should have been. It's something I've always regretted," he said.

Four years later, in 1972, Aspromonte replaced Alvin Dark (and interim manager Johnny Lipon) to pilot the Indians, a job he held

"I didn't realize until it was too late that it was my temper, my disposition that kept me from being the player I should have been."

---

for three seasons. At that time the American League was composed of two six-team divisions. The Indians, under Aspromonte, finished fifth (with a 72-84 record) in 1972, sixth (71-91) in 1973, and fourth (77-85) in 1974, after being in contention most of the season.

"You have to remember," he said, "that I took over a team that had equaled the worst losing season [60-102 in 1971] in franchise history, and we were rebuilding with a lot of young, unproven players," most of whom came up through the minors with Aspromonte.

The Aspromonte managerial era also took place during the Indians' financially stressed period, when there was little money to acquire—or even keep—good players. In fact, many often were sold or traded to meet the monthly payroll.

"When I was hired [as manager] it was pretty much understood that we needed five years to get the [rebuilding] job done right. I knew we needed to add at least one top pitcher or one top hitter, but they [principal owner Ted Bonda and General Manager Phil Seghi] decided otherwise and chose to go another way. A lot of it had to do with the fact they didn't have the money to spend for what we needed, or refused to spend the money that was necessary to get what we needed."

On September 12, 1974, with the Indians in second place with a 71-71 record, five games behind New York, they acquired Robinson, then a player for the Angels, though nobody, neither Bonda nor Seghi, informed Aspromonte until after the fact.

"It came out of the clear blue sky," said Aspromonte. "Seghi told me, 'Hey, slugger, I got you the right-handed hitter we've needed.' That's how I found out we got Robinson. About five minutes after Seghi told me, Robinson walked into the clubhouse."

The Indians went on to lose 14 of their final 20 games, winding up in fourth place, 14 games behind the Yankees. Exactly three weeks later, on October 3, 1974, Robinson was officially named manager of the Indians, replacing Aspromonte. *Officially,* because, from the very moment Seghi claimed Robinson on waivers from the Angels, speculation became rampant that he would become baseball's first black manager.

Afterwards, Aspromonte would be quoted as saying that the Indians "needed a fall guy for all the bad things that happened, and I was it."

Aspromonte, who turned 75 years old on September 22, 2006, and wife, Lorrie, were married in 1956. He and his brother Bob, who played 13 seasons (1956–71) with four National League teams, are retired from the beer business but remain active in real estate and "with our investments."

Aspromonte said he isn't sure where the game is headed, what with the ever-escalation of salaries as well as ever-increasing problems involving the use of performance-enhancing drugs by so many players.

"It's crazy . . . unbelievable," Aspromonte said of the salaries players are receiving today. "The most I ever made as a player was $25,000 in 1960 with the Indians, and I went from $40,000 as their manager in 1972, to $50,000 [each year] in 1973 and 1974.

"When I was a player they [owners] treated us like peasants, traded us and bought us and sold us and paid us the minimum whenever they could. But now the tail is wagging the dog, and it's the players who have too much power."

As for the steroids issue in professional sports today, Aspromonte said, "It's a huge problem. I can see the difference in the sizes of the players, although I don't think they are all taking steroids. But they are heavy on the body building.

"You go into a clubhouse today and it's bigger and better than any health club I ever saw. The players are really big boys now, and I can only assume that [the use of steroids] is one of the reasons.

"In my opinion, baseball is too lenient. The players union has stopped Mr. Selig from invoking stronger penalties."

Despite his concern for the health of the game, it is still a large part of his life.

"I loved baseball . . . I still do. I never lost that love, despite all that happened, all the disappointments," said Aspromonte.

"I will go to my grave thinking how thrilled I was to have been a major-league player, and that I was exceptionally gifted to have the chance to be a major-league manager. There are only a few of us who can say that, and I am proud, very proud, of that."

JOE
AZCUE

Catcher, 1963–69

Best season: 1963, 94 games, .284 batting average, 14 home runs, 46 RBI

Indians career: 594 games, .266 avg., 45 home runs, 229 RBI

He was only a "throw-in" when the Indians acquired him on May 25, 1963, but he quickly became "immortal"—as in, "The Immortal Cuban"—if only temporarily. That's the nickname Joe Azcue was given shortly after his arrival from Kansas City, along with short-stop Dick Howser in a deal for catcher Doc Edwards and $100,000.

Eventually, of course, Azcue proved to be merely mortal. Ah, but back there in the midst of the bad old days of Indians baseball, Azcue was indeed something special most of that 1963 season. Not only did he do everything right to earn that "immortal" nickname, he also seemed even then to be a lock to eventually make it to the Hall of Fame.

Well, *almost*.

"Don't ask me . . . I don't know either," is the way Azcue answered the obvious question about his amazing debut in Cleveland as a 23-year-old catcher.

The truth be told, Azcue—the throw in who became a "steal" for the Tribe—was included with Howser only to balance the deal and play behind the Tribe's regular receiver, John Romano. For the pre-vious seven years, Azcue had been toiling without much success in the minor leagues, after failing trials with Kansas City in 1962 and Cincinnati in 1960.

Howser was the key player in the trade, as evidenced by the fact that the Indians, despite their financial instability at the time, sent $100,000—to balance the deal. It was one of the few times they had money and/or were willing to spend it to acquire a player they really wanted.

The Kansas City team, the Athletics franchise that later moved to Oakland, thought Azcue wouldn't hit enough in the big leagues and wanted Edwards, who'd been playing behind Romano in Cleveland. Hence the trade, which pleased everybody, especially Azcue, who was unhappy the way he was being treated by A's owner Charley Finley.

"[Finley] didn't like me, and I didn't like him," Azcue said of his relationship with the often-obnoxious Kansas City owner. "He got mad at me because I didn't hit so good when [the A's] gave me a chance in 1962. I told him, 'Mr. Finley, the reason I am not hitting so good is because I have worms.'"

Worms?

"Yes, worms in my stomach," said Azcue. "I lost a lot of weight . . . I was weak . . . but I tried to play anyway. I didn't tell anybody I was sick, but I couldn't play good and they sent me to [Class AAA] Portland. I was mad, but then I was glad."

Glad because he was still in Portland in 1963 when he was traded to the Indians, said Azcue, from his home in Overland Park, Kansas.

Azcue and his wife, Judy, a Kansas City girl he married in 1962, raised three daughters: Angela, Michelle and Melanie. He is the manager of the detail shop of an automobile dealership, for which he has worked since 1985.

On that fateful day in 1963 when he joined the Tribe after spending most of the previous night in airports and on a plane, Azcue fell asleep in the bullpen. It was during a game against the Washington Senators in Cleveland's Municipal Stadium.

"How did we not win a couple of pennants, or at least do better with the great starting pitchers we had in those years?"

———————————————

As luck would have it, while Azcue snoozed, Romano was hit with a foul tip and suffered two broken bones in his right hand. Suddenly, Azcue became the Indians' regular catcher—if only, as was thought at the time—until Romano could return to duty. But Azcue caught fire. He got 17 hits, including several game winners, in his first 40 at-bats for a .425 average, and the Indians won 18 of the first 21 games with their new catcher, boosting them to within 3½ games of first place.

The Immortal Cuban came back to earth later in the season—as did the Indians, who wound up in fifth place—though Azcue still finished with a respectable .284 average, 14 homers, and 46 RBI in 94 games. And because Azcue established himself as the Indians' regular catcher, the Indians traded Romano the following winter in a three-team deal on January 20, 1965, that returned fan-favorite Rocky Colavito to Cleveland.

When Azcue looks back at his six-plus seasons with the Tribe he admits it is with puzzlement. "How did we not win a couple of pennants, or at least do better, with the great starting pitchers we had in those years?" he wondered.

During his time in Cleveland the Indians never finished higher than third, which they did in 1968, but they still were 16½ games out at the end of the season.

"I still can't believe it," he said. "You tell me who had a better starting staff than we did [in 1966–68]. We didn't have the middle relievers we needed, but we had four of the best starters in baseball."

Those would be Sam McDowell, Luis Tiant, Sonny Siebert, and Steve Hargan. Especially McDowell.

"I would like to write a book about Sam," said Azcue. "He was a good pitcher . . . no, I mean a *very* good pitcher . . . OK, a *helluva* pitcher. He threw harder than anybody I ever caught, or anybody I ever batted against. Sam had everything. The best fastball, the best curveball, the best slider, and the best change-up I ever caught." And then, chuckling, Azcue said, "He also had a great spitball when he wanted to throw it."

He recalled an incident from 1964, when McDowell was promoted from Portland and Birdie Tebbetts was the Indians manager.

"Before Sam's first game—it was against the Yankees—Birdie called us into his office and told Sam, 'If you throw anything except a fastball or change-up, it will cost you $100,'" related Azcue. "So, we followed Birdie's orders, only fastballs and change-ups, and Sam shut out the Yankees on two hits, even though they figured out what was happening.

"Yogi Berra came up to the plate in the eighth inning and said, 'Geez, Joe, we know what's coming and we still can't hit it. The kid is too tough.'

"Tiant was very good, too. He just threw whatever he wanted . . . we didn't use any signals. I always knew what was coming because I knew him so well. He didn't have anything that could fool me."

Azcue's favorite memories in baseball were the two no-hitters he caught, for Siebert (on June 10, 1966) and Clyde Wright, then of the Angels (on July 3, 1970).

"I didn't call a pitch for Siebert either," he said. "I told him, 'Just throw whatever you like,' so he did, and nobody could hit it."

Another favorite—because it was so funny, but could have been disastrous—was a time (Azcue doesn't remember when it happened) that he forgot to put on his mask when he went behind the plate in a game. Nobody noticed until after the first batter was retired. Azcue said, "Oh, my God, I could've been killed."

He grew up in Cienfuegos, Cuba, and came to the United States in 1955, when he was 16 years old. "My signing bonus [with Cincinnati] was a catcher's mitt they said cost $75," he said. "But that was OK, because it was all I wanted."

Azcue's peak salary in baseball was $26,000 in 1969. "It's great that players are making so much money today . . . except they are not worth it," he said. "But I don't blame them for taking it. I would do the same thing if the owners wanted to pay me.

"It proves what we thought back in my day, that [the owners] were making a lot more money than they admitted.

"But it's not just the money that's different. In my day we used to go out to dinner with you guys [in the media] and talk about the game and stuff like that. We were like one big, happy family. We had fun. But now, the players say the hell with you guys, or they go into the trainer's room and hide if they did not have a good game."

Azcue remained with the Indians through the first couple of weeks of 1969, when, no longer "immortal" in Cleveland, he was traded to Boston. He retired in 1972 after also playing for California and Milwaukee.

And though his major-league statistics are those of a mere mortal—a .252 batting average, 50 home runs, 304 RBI—he'll long be remembered for the headlines he earned back in 1963.

RICHIE
SCHEINBLUM

Outfielder, 1965, 1967–69

Best season: 1967, 18 games,
.318 batting average, 0 home runs,
6 RBI

Indians career: 143 games,
.218 avg., 1 home runs, 24 RBI

When he was signed as an amateur free agent in 1964 and given a $12,000 bonus, Richie Scheinblum was considered by the Indians to be one of their outstanding prospects and was expected to reach major-league stardom.

But it never happened. Not in Cleveland, though he did well elsewhere.

It might have been different—better—for Scheinblum had it been possible to divide the baseball season into two parts, the first being the month of April, and the second being the next five months, May through September.

"That would've helped," acknowledged Scheinblum from his home in Palm Harbor, Florida, where he is in sales for CorpLogo-Wear, a company that produces promotional products.

"I was one of the worst hitters in April that ever played the game," Scheinblum said.

"It seemed that, if I could get through the month of April, I was OK. Aprils kind of destroyed me. Don't ask me why. I never figured it out. Maybe because I always dreamed of playing in the big leagues and, especially early in my career, I was a little stunned, over-awed that I was suddenly playing with a guy like Rocky Colavito. He grew up in the same New York neighborhood that I did, and playing with him was like seeing my baseball card come to life."

The records during Scheinblum's four partial seasons (1965, 1967–69) with the Indians bear out his contention. It was especially bad in 1969. After he won the starting right-field position, Scheinblum went hitless in the Tribe's opener and didn't get his first hit until he'd gone 0-for-35.

"It was horrible," he said. "I wasn't helping the team, and I surely wasn't helping myself. I wasn't striking out and I was hitting the ball hard, but nothing would fall in. It was like the Stadium was too big for me. When I finally did get a hit, I heard that my batting average at the time [.028] was the lowest, other than three zeroes, ever posted on the Stadium scoreboard.

"Somebody also told me I broke the major-league record for 0-fers, which had been 0-for-28 by Willie Mays and Nellie Fox, and both of them are in the Hall of Fame.

"I should have known it was going to be a bad season because of what happened in spring training," he said. "One day I hit for the negative cycle—I got thrown out at first base, I got thrown out at second base trying for a double, I got thrown out at third base trying for a triple, and I got thrown out at home trying for an inside-the-park homer, all in the same game."

He finished the 1969 season with a .186 average that included one homer and 13 RBI in 102 games.

Scheinblum went on to play eight years in the major leagues. After his contract was sold by the Tribe, he played with the Washington Senators in 1971, Kansas City in 1972, Cincinnati and California in 1973, and finally the Angels, Royals, and St. Louis in 1974.

Unfortunately for the Indians, and also for Richie, he never lived up to expectations in Cleveland, although three years later, in 1972, he came close to winning the American League batting championship. That was the season Scheinblum's average was at the top of the A.L. in early September and, with two weeks remaining, he and Rod Carew were tied at .340. "At that time nobody else was even hitting .300," he recalled.

"I was one of the worst hitters in April that ever played the game."

———————————

Then, in a game in Oakland, Scheinblum fouled a pitch off his ankle. It was bad enough that he had to be carried off the field, though he was back in the lineup the next game. "I wanted to finish the season, which I shouldn't have done because my ankle was still sore and I couldn't run very well." As a result, he said, "I was thrown out at first base eight times from left field—*left field!*—during those final two weeks."

By the time the season ended, Scheinblum's average fell to an even .300 (135-for-450 in 134 games), while Carew went on to win his second (of seven) batting titles with a .318 mark. "Rod had 55 infield hits that season, and I had none, zero," said Scheinblum, who includes Carew as one of his best friends. "Every time we get together at his house I look at his 1972 award and tell him, 'That one's mine—or should have been.'"

Scheinblum hit .235 in 106 games with the Reds and Angels in 1973, and in 1974 he batted .183 in 52 games with the Angels, Royals, and Cardinals.

When St. Louis wanted to trade him to the Los Angeles Dodgers, Scheinblum requested and received his release. "It was a mistake. I know that now, although at the time I didn't want to play for the Dodgers. I grew up in the Bronx, and I hated the [Brooklyn] Dodgers."

So, instead of going to Los Angeles, Scheinblum signed to play for the Hiroshima Carp in Japan in 1975 and 1976. He called it "a fabulous experience" and batted over .300 each season.

He was paid $130,000 over the two seasons, which represented a huge increase over the largest salary Scheinblum earned in the major leagues—$36,000 in 1973.

The year he returned from Japan, major leaguers received the right to become free agents and to sell their services to the highest bidders. It was too late for Scheinblum, however, who was 34 years old and hobbled after suffering a severed Achilles' tendon in his right leg that required him to wear a brace for seven months.

The injury happened while playing in a pickup basketball game that winter (1976–77) in the Anaheim, California, area where Scheinblum and his wife began a jewelry business, which they operated for 12 years. They were married in 1966 and divorced in 1992, after which Scheinblum moved to Florida, where he is close to several other former players, including Dick Bosman and Bert Blyleven.

Scheinblum, who is the godfather of Blyleven's son Tim, is active in golf after giving up the game temporarily because of a second hip replacement in 2002. He also pays close attention to the progress his son Monty is making as a professional golfer.

The fondest memory of Scheinblum's career was playing right field in the 1972 All-Star Game in Atlanta. "I was 0-for-1, but I'll never forget how thrilling it was just to be there with all those great players.

"Something else I'll never forget is how the fans cheered—for at least 20 minutes without stopping, and the whole stadium shook—when Hank Aaron hit a two-run homer. It gave me goose bumps."

And the lowlight of his career?

"You shouldn't even have to ask," he said. "It was the 0-fer streak. But I've got to tell you, it wasn't really 0-for-35. When I was 0-for-28, or 0-for-29, the official scorer could have—should have, everybody in our dugout said—given me a hit instead of charging the fielder with an error. I still remember it very well. I also remember the official scorer very well."

Then he laughed and said, "But I forgive you."

(Author's note: The name of the official scorer who didn't give Scheinblum the hit that would have reduced his 0-fer streak to 28 or 29, and raised his .186 average that season to .191, is on the cover of this book.)

RON
HASSEY

Catcher, 1978–84

Best season: 1980, 130 games,
.318 batting average, 8 home runs,
65 RBI

Indians career: 569 games,
.271 avg., 26 home runs, 226 RBI

There aren't many—hardly *any*—jobs in baseball that Ron Hassey hasn't held since his retirement in 1991 after 14 seasons as a major-league catcher.

Hassey wasn't timid when he played—for the Tribe, Chicago Cubs, New York Yankees, Chicago White Sox, Oakland and Montreal—and he isn't timid about expressing his next goal.

"I've done just about everything except manage in the big leagues," he said. "I played, coached, scouted, worked in the front office, was a field coordinator, and managed in the minor leagues. I think I'm well prepared to manage in the big leagues."

Hassey owns a distinction not shared by anybody in the history of major-league baseball: He's the only man to have caught two of the 15 perfect games ever pitched.

The first was Len Barker's gem for the Indians on May 15, 1981, against Toronto; the other was by Dennis Martinez for the Expos on July 28, 1991, against Los Angeles.

Hassey didn't become a catcher until he was a senior at the University of Arizona in 1976, when the Wildcats won the NCAA national championship. Shortly thereafter he was selected by the Indians in the 18th round of the amateur draft.

"Everybody who's played in the big leagues remembers the date he was called up from the minors. There was nothing like it."

He'd been a shortstop and previously was drafted out of high school by Cincinnati, but he chose to accept a scholarship to Arizona, located in his hometown of Tucson. The coach who switched Hassey from shortstop to catcher was Jerry Kindall, a former major-league second baseman who played for the Indians from 1962 to 1964.

The Indians signed Hassey for $1,000, which was $2,000 less than the Reds had offered four years earlier. He climbed through the minors in two seasons and was called up by the Indians on April 16, 1978.

Hassey calls his promotion to the big leagues the highlight of his career, above the distinction of catching two perfect games and even above being in the World Series three times with Oakland (1988–90) and being on the winning team in 1989.

"Everybody who's played in the big leagues remembers the date he was called up from the minors. For me, there was nothing like it," he said. "It's something my dad [Bill] always wanted but never got, and something that my wife [Jennifer] and I hope our son Brad gets one of these days."

Bill Hassey, a former outfielder, played several years in the minors for the Yankees but never reached the majors. Brad Hassey, born in 1979, an infielder who also graduated from the University of Arizona, was a 19th-round selection of the Toronto Blue Jays in 2002. He played in the Class AA Eastern League in 2006.

Hassey earned his peak salary in 1989. "It was about $900,000, including bonuses, which I thought was pretty good," he said, although it's not even close to the current *average* major- league salary, which climbed to well over $2 million in 2006.

Since hanging up his catcher's glove—and the so-called "tools of ignorance"—Hassey said he has prepared himself for the major-league managerial job he hopes to get eventually by having accomplished "everything in baseball that I wanted to do, and everything that I felt I had to do."

He started in 1992 as an advance scout for the Yankees, was a coach for the Colorado Rockies from 1993 to 1995, was Tony LaRussa's bench coach for the St. Louis Cardinals in 1996, returned to scouting in 1997 with the Arizona Diamondbacks to help them prepare for the National League expansion draft, then served as special assistant to the Diamondbacks' general manager Joe Garagiola Jr. in 1998 and 1999. He then was the Diamondbacks' minor-league field coordinator from 2000 to 2003, a minor-league manager for the Florida Marlins in 2004, and returned to the big leagues in 2005 as bench coach in Seattle under former teammate Mike Hargrove.

Hassey's memories of Barker's and Martinez's perfect games are still vivid, and he spoke with surprising candor—and simplicity—of the role he played. "They threw the ball. I only caught it for them," he said.

Recalling Barker's 3-0 victory over the Blue Jays, Hassey answered the obvious question: "To tell you the truth, I wasn't nervous. When it ended I didn't even know it was a perfect game. I knew it was a no-hitter, we all did. But who would ever think Lennie Barker would pitch a game without walking anybody? It was amazing to me because, frankly, Lennie was more of a thrower than a pitcher.

"But that night he was throwing his fastball in the zone, and his curve was like a ball falling off a table, which he also kept in the strike zone. It was sort of a curve-slider, and a lot of times it broke in the dirt, but guys were swinging at it."

Of Martinez's 2-0 victory over the Dodgers 10 years later, Hassey said, "It was completely different. Martinez was a pitcher's pitcher. He knew what he wanted to do and how he was going to do it. He was not a power pitcher, not by any means, and he had to have good control and be able to hit his spots to be effective.

"When I went to Montreal [in 1991] and started to catch Martinez, I think he tried to fool the batter and the catcher—me. No pitcher I ever caught shook off [my signals] the way he did, although, after a while, he started to understand me, what I was trying to get him to do. I guess I finally earned his trust.

"He and I got along well by the end of the season, though I admit we didn't at the beginning. I didn't really object to him shaking me off so much the first four or five times I caught him, but I didn't like it. No catcher would."

In Martinez's perfect game, Hassey said, "he dominated the Dodgers as much as Barker did [the Blue Jays], but in a different way because he was more of a control pitcher. Barker's fastball was in the 94 to 95 [mph] range, and he could get away with a pitch that wasn't where he wanted it. Martinez's fastball was anywhere from 88 to 90, and he had to hit his spots. That night [against the Dodgers] he did.

"I was very lucky to have caught a lot of very good pitchers," said Hassey. Included among them was Phil Niekro with the Yankees in 1985—although he admitted, "Catching him was a nightmare. I could hit a knuckleball, but I couldn't catch one.

"Billy Martin [then the Yankees' manager] used to say said that I had to know everybody in the box seats behind home plate because I was back there so much retrieving passed balls."

Hassey chose his words carefully on the steroids issue now so prevalent in baseball. "Before I express an opinion about how to handle the records that [Barry] Bonds and others achieve, I'd have to learn more about what steroids do for a player. Do they really enhance a player's ability to hit a baseball? Probably so. But one thing I do know for sure, despite all the comments and speculation, you still have to have great hand-eye coordination to hit a baseball."

Hassey called his six-plus seasons with the Indians "very lean years." He was right. "One year we'd have speed, the next year we didn't. One year we'd have pitching but no hitting, and the next year we'd have hitting but no pitching. And there always seemed to be a financial problem. We weren't drawing anybody, but then the club wasn't putting a good product on the field, and I couldn't blame the fans.

"The ballpark [Municipal Stadium] wasn't very nice, but it didn't bother me. There were problems—the Stadium was big and cold and smelled bad sometimes—but it had a lot of tradition, and I liked it. But again, for me, just being in the big leagues made it good."

Eventually, he hopes, it'll get even better—when a major-league managerial job becomes available for him.

RICK
WAITS

Pitcher, 1975–83

Best season: 1979, 34 games,
16-13 won-lost record, 0 saves,
4.44 ERA

Indians career: 235 games,
74-84 won-lost record, 3 saves,
4.18 ERA

Rick Waits never heard from Bucky Dent, the former Yankees shortstop he helped make a hero nearly three decades ago.

But then, Waits never responded to the "probably over a thousand" letters he received from overjoyed—though only for a day—Boston Red Sox fans who, 24 hours later, were devastated, thanks to the heroics of the same Bucky Dent. It all relates to what Waits calls "the number-one thing," the highlight of his 12-year major-league pitching career, nine seasons of which were spent with the Indians.

"It's the time I beat the Yankees [9-2] in the last game of the 1978 season," said Waits, who now works for the "other" New York team, the Mets.

That victory by Waits, his 13th of the season, dropped the Yankees into a tie with Boston, which had beaten Toronto, 7-6, earlier in the day, forcing a playoff for the American League East championship.

New York won the next day, 5-4, on Dent's three-run homer. They went on to beat A.L. West champion Kansas City for the pennant, vaulting the Yankees into the World Series, which they won against Los Angeles.

"If we hadn't beaten the Yankees that day, Dent never would've had the chance to be a hero—and to this day he hasn't paid me a penny," Waits said, facetiously, of course.

The red-haired, left-handed ex-pitcher, who also was noted for his singing voice, spoke of October 1, 1978, the day that the Indians prevailed, nearly breaking the hearts of the Yankees and their fans—before Dent broke the hearts of the Red Sox and their fans.

As Waits recalled, "We were way out of it [in sixth place, 29 games behind] and had no place to go except home after the game, and the Yankees knew they had to win or face a sudden-death playoff in Boston. Yankee Stadium was filled with 55,000 screaming fans, and [future Hall of Famer] Catfish Hunter was on the mound against us. I pitched a complete game, a five-hitter, and wrapped it up by striking out the last two batters.

"But it wasn't me alone. Joe Charboneau and Andre Thornton hit home runs, all of our guys pounded the ball, and we played great defense. I had great stuff, but it really was a team effort.

"I remember how loud the fans were, and how quiet they became when the game ended. There wasn't much feedback, not at all, not from the Yankees. But for the next four or five days I got letters, probably over a thousand, from fans in New England. They obviously were mailed right after we beat the Yankees, and before the Red Sox played the game that Dent won with his homer."

It didn't bother Waits, he said, to have (almost) knocked the Yankees out of the division championship. "It's my theory that it doesn't matter who you play or what's on the line, you play just as hard to win all the time. It's a matter of pride, and you owe it to your team and your fans." Still, he admits, "There always was something special about beating the Yankees when you played for the Indians. None of us liked the Yankees, and I suppose it's the same now."

Beating the Yankees in the Tribe's 1978 finale gave Waits back-to-back victories—though they were six months apart—to further highlight his career.

The following season, in the Indians' home opener on April 7,

1979, Waits came within one pitch of hurling a no-hitter. Ironically, it was against the same Red Sox whose hopes he'd kept alive (for a day) the previous October. In his 3-0 victory over Boston in front of 47,231 fans in Cleveland's old Municipal Stadium, Jerry Remy got the only Red Sox hit, a sixth-inning single.

"I don't remember the pitch he hit, but it was a clean hit down the left field line, and I have no second thoughts about it," said Waits, who walked six batters and struck out four. He went on to win nine of his first 13 decisions in 1979 and wound up with a 16-13 won-lost record that included eight complete games and three shutouts.

"Almost everything clicked for me that year . . . maybe the one-hitter was an omen, an omen of good things to come," said Waits, who has worked for the Mets since 1995, currently as their minor-league pitching coordinator.

He is in charge of all the pitchers and pitching decisions among the Mets' seven farm clubs and two academies (in the Dominican Republic and in Venezuela).

"I've written the manual on how we pitch so that all our minor-league people, managers, coaches, and pitchers, are on the same page, doing the same things," he said.

"I enjoy what I'm doing, but I'd like to be a major-league pitching coach down the road. Getting back to the big leagues after you retire as a player is kind of a reward for the hard work you've done. On the other hand, in the big leagues you don't get to teach as much, and I consider myself to be primarily a teacher, which I love doing."

Waits makes his home in Tucson, Arizona, with his wife, Annie, whom he married in 1979. They have three children: a daughter, Elizabeth, who attends law school and has a summer job at the Pentagon; and two sons—Michael, who graduated from Wheaton College with a major in microbiology, and John, who attends college in Argentina.

"All of our kids spent a year abroad before starting college—Elizabeth in Paris, Michael in Bologna, Italy, and John in Buenos Aires," said Waits.

"[Coaching] in the big leagues, you don't get to teach as much, and I consider myself to be primarily a teacher, which I love doing."

Waits's peak salary in baseball was $460,000 with Milwaukee in 1985, his final season. After retiring from the Brewers he went to Italy, where he pitched for and managed professional teams for five years, winning three national championships.

The caliber of baseball in Italy, Waits said, is about the level of Class AA and high Class A in the United States. He pitched and managed in Rimini, a town near Venice, and in Parma, located near Milan.

"The American military brought baseball to Italy during World War II, and the Italian people love the game," he said. "I enjoyed being involved, and though I didn't make much money, neither did I have to spend much."

Waits began his baseball career when he was selected in the fifth round of the 1970 amateur draft and received a signing bonus of $21,000 from the Washington Senators (who became the Texas Rangers in 1972). He languished in the minor leagues for 5½ seasons, getting only one chance—for one inning in 1973—in the major leagues with the Rangers.

Finally, on June 13, 1975, two days before what was then the trading deadline, the Indians acquired him, along with pitchers Jim Bibby and Jackie Brown, plus $100,000, for Gaylord Perry, who was not getting along with manager Frank Robinson. It proved to be a good deal for the Tribe, and especially for Waits.

"It was the first real chance I got to pitch in the big leagues," he said. "I didn't even get to pitch an inning [for the Rangers] in spring training in 1975. I was at the point where I didn't know what I had to do."

Then, of course, came the trade to Cleveland, and Waits eventually became the fourth winningest left-handed pitcher in Indians history, behind Sam McDowell (with 122 victories), C.C. Sabathia (who's still active), and Joe Shaute (who won 78 games from 1922 to 1930).

Waits's won-lost record was 74-84 in his seven full seasons and two partial seasons with the Indians, who never finished higher than fourth (twice), were fifth, sixth (four times), and seventh (twice), and never won more than 81 games while he was with them.

And of those 74 victories by Waits, two were especially memorable, one that temporarily broke the hearts of the Yankees and their fans, and the other that came within one pitch of putting him on the list of major-league pitchers who threw no-hitters.

FRED
WHITFIELD

First Baseman, 1963–67

Best season: 1965, 132 games, .293 batting average, 26 home runs, 90 RBI

Indians career: 579 games, .257 avg., 93 home runs, 282 RBI

The voice on the other end of the telephone asked, "You remember when me and Larry Brown and some of the guys used to get that guitar out in the clubhouse and sing?"

Affirmative.

Then the man drawled, "I don't see much of any of the old guys anymore, but I'm still doing a lot of singing. And now, I get paid for it."

The voice belonged to Fred Whitfield, a.k.a. "Wingy," speaking from Gadsden, Alabama, where he lives in retirement—make that "semi-retirement," he wanted it said—since the early 1990s.

"We formed a gospel group and go around and sing in nursing homes and churches, places like that, two or three times a week."

"We" are Whitfield and his wife, Helen, one of their five sons, Fred Jr., Helen's sister Susie, and Susie's boyfriend.

Whitfield played nine years in the major leagues, including five with the Indians (1963-67). He was a first baseman because, well, as he said, "Because that was the only position I could play . . . I didn't have too many tools, but I could hit a little bit and I always tried hard."

Even before joining the Tribe in a trade with St. Louis, Whitfield was called "Wingy" because he had a weak (left) throwing arm, which he readily acknowledged. It prevented him from playing any position other than first base.

"One of my minor-league managers told me, 'You've got a chicken wing for an arm,' and he was right. I threw my arm out in high school when the coach asked me to pitch, and in those days when a coach wanted you to do something, you did it.

"The next day I could hardly throw a ball from first base to home plate, and my arm never got much better. It was always bad . . . still is," he said.

In addition to being known as Wingy, Whitfield also was called "a Yankee Killer," a nickname he liked better, he said, "Because I loved to beat those damn Yankees," which he often did with his bat.

"One year, I think it was 1965, I hit 10 homers off the Yankees in 18 games. I had pretty good luck against them. I was just blessed, I guess."

Then another reason came to mind. "I always wanted to show [Yankees manager] Johnny Keane that he made a mistake about me."

Keane had been the manager of the Cardinals when Whitfield was a major-league rookie in 1962. "At the end of that season they wanted me to play winter ball, but I wanted to go back home to my farm [in Vandiver, Alabama]. That's when they got rid of me," and traded him to the Indians.

Whitfield began his professional baseball career in Pittsburgh's farm system in 1956 when he was 18, but he didn't last long with the Pirates. Only about two weeks.

"They signed me as an outfielder, but when they saw that I wasn't too swift a runner and couldn't throw very good, they released me in spring training," he said.

The Baltimore Orioles signed Whitfield in 1957, but that trial didn't last long either.

"They liked my bat, but not my arm," he said.

It was his bat that earned Whitfield another trial in 1958, this time with the Cardinals, who gave him a $500 signing bonus. "I thought I was in high cotton when they gave me all that money just to play ball," he said. "Pittsburgh also gave me $500 to sign, but when they sent me home they wanted the money back. I finally got to keep it, but not without a big argument with the scout."

He climbed through the Cardinals' farm system, and when Bill White, their all-star first baseman, was injured early in 1962, Whitfield was called up and batted .266 with 8 homers in 73 games. When White returned, Whitfield was deemed expendable.

In his five seasons in Cleveland, Whitfield hit for a combined .257 average with a total of 93 homers, but became expendable again when the Indians acquired Tony Horton in June 1967. He was traded to Cincinnati where he played in 1968 and 1969, and ended his career with the Expos in 1970.

"When [Montreal] let me go, I was ready to go," said Wingy. "I was tired of baseball, and my wife was tired of me traveling and being away from home so much, though we both liked it when I played in Cleveland."

Whitfield returned to Alabama and worked for 23 years as a shipping clerk for a company that manufactured electrical products. He and Helen raised sons Max, Ted, Fred Jr., Jeff, and Derek, and daughter Tammy.

"All the boys played baseball, and a couple of them were pretty good. One was a shortstop and another was a first baseman like me, except that he could throw. But neither got a chance to play pro ball. It seems to me the scouts down here don't have any sense, but I guess it worked out pretty well because all my boys are doing OK," said Whitfield.

"My third oldest son, Ted, is a preacher, and I'd rather him doing that than anything else. All the other boys have good jobs, too, so they're probably better off than if they were playing ball."

Whitfield said he doesn't pay much attention to baseball anymore and is surprised how much money players are paid today.

"Most of them are millionaires, and if they have a hangnail or a sore toe and don't feel like playing, they just tell you guys [the media], 'Don't talk to me, talk to my agent.' Shoot, I didn't even know what an agent was.

"It looks to me like [fans] are being priced out of the stands because the owners have to pay the players so much money. The cost of tickets keeps going up so high that a family can't afford to go to a game unless they have $250 or $300 to spend.

"Every year it seems they get worse—or better. Worse if you're a fan buying the tickets, and better if you're a player getting all that money."

Whitfield's highest salary was $28,000 in 1966, after his best season with the Indians, when he hit .293 with 26 homers and 90 RBI. It represented a $5,000 raise.

"I had to fight like hell to get that much out of Gabe Paul," Whitfield said. "He didn't want to pay anybody, but then, I guess [the Indians] didn't have much money either.

"I guess I was just born at the wrong time. When I started [in the minor leagues] I got a dollar-and-a-half meal money every day. I mean, that was for the whole day. But the way things are now, from what I can tell, maybe it was better back then, except for the money, so maybe I was born at the right time, I'm not sure.

"It might have been better for all of us back then because we appreciated it more than it seems the players do now. But I don't care. I don't let it bother me any. My family is doing good, and we're happy.

"Tell Brownie [Larry Brown] and Maxie [Max Alvis] that I'm doing OK. My health is good, and I've got almost as much hair as I did when we sat around and sang country songs in the old days.

"And if they want to come down and join our gospel group, I'll be here with my guitar waiting for them."

JIM
BIBBY

Pitcher, 1975–77

Best season: 1976, 34 games,
13-7 won-lost record, 1 save,
3.20 ERA

Indians career: 95 games,
30-29 won-lost record, 4 saves,
3.36 ERA

"The Lord has blessed us," said Jackie Bibby, the wife of former Indians pitcher Jim Bibby, who recently fought and apparently is winning the toughest battle of his life.

In October 2005, Bibby was diagnosed with multiple myeloma, which Jackie described as "a form of bone marrow cancer," and underwent a successful stem cell transplant.

"Everything went well and Jim is doing fine, though he must undergo examination and evaluation every two or three months," she said from their home in Lynchburg, Virginia. Jim and Jackie, who teaches in middle school, have been married since 1968 and raised two daughters, Tanya and Tamara.

Jim retired in 1984 after 12 years in the major leagues compiling a 111-101 won-lost record, then was a minor-league pitching coach the next 15 years.

After he was signed by the New York Mets as an amateur free agent in 1965 at the age of 20 and pitched that season at Marion, Virginia, of the rookie Appalachian League, Bibby was drafted by Uncle Sam. He spent the next two years in the army in Vietnam, and missed the entire 1970 season when he underwent spinal fusion surgery.

The Mets traded Bibby to St. Louis in October 1971. He was dealt to Texas in June 1973, and two years later, in 1975, he became a member of the Indians. But the Tribe lost him after 2½ seasons because of a "simple misunderstanding"—although, actually, it was more simply a case of the Tribe being financially strapped.

The problem arose in October 1977 and—unfortunately for the Indians—was settled five months later, on March 6, 1978, when Bibby was the winner of a major decision by an arbitrator and declared a free agent. It enabled him to auction his services and, subsequently, develop and expand his career into one of the best in baseball.

It was Indians general manager Phil Seghi who called it a "simple misunderstanding," an innocent oversight that could have happened to anybody, though the arbitrator, Alexander B. Porter, didn't agree.

The issue: the failure by the Tribe to pay Bibby a $10,000 incentive bonus he earned by starting 30 games in 1977.

The Indians, through attorney Armond Arnson, claimed they had the money and were ready, willing, and able to meet their financial obligation. They also argued that they had the approval of Bibby and his agent, Richard Hull of Dallas, to delay the payment that was due October 3. But Hull denied any agreement had been made, and the arbitrator ruled that the Indians were in default.

It turned out to be one of the best things that could have happened in Bibby's career. It also turned out to be one of the worst things that could have happened to the Indians, especially at that time when, as often was the case back then, they were in dire need of pitching.

With the loss of Bibby, the 1978 staff was composed of Rick Waits, Rick Wise, Mike Paxton, Don Hood, and David Clyde—and all but Waits and Hood were newcomers to the team. Only Waits had been a starter in 1977, when his won-lost record was 9-7 for the Tribe. Hood was on the team in 1977 but, while appearing in 41 games, started only five.

"Leaving Cleveland gave me a chance to go to a better ball club, get to the World Series, and make some money."

The arbitrator's ruling was issued on March 6, 1978, more than five months after Bibby posted a 12-13 won-lost record for the Tribe in 1977. He was 13-7 in 1976.

The incentive-bonus clause was part of Bibby's two-year contract that ran through the 1978 season.

Ironically, by design or coincidence, Bibby didn't make that bonus-clinching 30th start until the final day of 1977. He did so in the opener of a double header, an otherwise meaningless game between the Indians and Toronto. Manager Jeff Torborg took Bibby out of the bullpen, where he'd been assigned—again, by design or coincidence—since early September, and started him against the Blue Jays.

Bibby had been acquired by the Indians in a June 13, 1975, trade with Texas for Gaylord Perry in a deal in which the Rangers also sent pitchers Jackie Brown and Waits, and $100,000 to Cleveland.

In the wake of the arbitrator's ruling, offers to sign Bibby came rolling in from several clubs. Nine days later, on March 15, he agreed to a one-year contract with Pittsburgh for $200,000.

With the Indians in 1977, Bibby's salary was $83,000 (as it also would have been in 1978). "It was the most I ever made in baseball—until Seghi screwed up and I signed with the Pirates," he said. "I was glad to get the contract from the Pirates, but there was no animosity on my part against Cleveland. There might have been by Seghi, but I don't know."

Animosity or not, Bibby made it clear that the arbitrator's decision that freed him from the Indians was "the best thing that ever happened to me in baseball."

Bear in mind, 1978 was only the second year of free agency. At that time the average salary in the major leagues was $97,800, the median salary was $68,000, and the minimum was $21,000. Since then, the average has escalated to well over $2 million, and the minimum to $327,000.

"Leaving Cleveland was a good opportunity because it gave me a chance to go to a better ball club, get to the World Series, and make some money," said Bibby. "I enjoyed my time in Cleveland, but there were certain things that just didn't work out for me at the time . . . things I don't want to get into."

The Pirates won the National League pennant in 1979, when Bibby went 12-4 with a 2.81 earned run average. He started two games without a decision as Pittsburgh beat Baltimore in seven games in the World Series, after which he collected a winner's share of $28,236.87.

"With the Pirates, the thing of it is, they were the best team I ever played for, and I won most of my games [50 with 32 losses] there, they scored a lot of runs for me, not like Cleveland and Texas, and got me a World Series ring.

"I was an under-.500 pitcher until I went to Pittsburgh, and because I did, I wound up with a good career. I won over 100 games and led the National League in winning percentage [19-6, .760] in 1980)."

Even before going to Pittsburgh, he pitched a no-hitter and one one-hitter. "And because of the no-hitter, I've at least got my cap in the Hall of Fame," he said.

Bibby's no-hitter was a 6-0 victory for the Rangers against Oakland on July 30, 1973. His one-hitter for Pittsburgh, on May 19, 1981 against Atlanta, was not only a near no-hitter but almost a perfect game. Bibby retired 27 consecutive batters after the Braves' Terry Harper led off the game with a single in the Pirates' 5-0 victory. Bibby also pitched a one-hitter against Kansas City for Texas on June 29, 1973.

It was shortly after that one-hitter against the Royals that Bibby suffered a rotator cuff injury that eventually ended his career. He finished the 1981 season with a 6-3 record, missed all of 1982, and went 5-12 with the Pirates in 1983. He tried to continue with Texas in 1984 but wasn't successful, appearing in eight games for the Rangers without a decision. Later in 1984 he signed with St. Louis but didn't pitch.

Now, as he continues his recovery from multiple myeloma and the stem cell transplant, Bibby plays golf "almost every day," has a handicap of "about eight or ten," and, at six five and 250 pounds, hits the ball "pretty far . . . sometimes so far I can't find it—though it depends on how far I can kick it when nobody is looking," he said.

"I think I'm doing OK . . . I feel good . . . and my wife is right," he said. "We've been blessed."

WAYNE
GARLAND

Pitcher, 1977–81

Best season: 1977, 38 games,
13-19 won-lost record, 0 saves,
3.60 ERA

Indians career: 99 games,
28-48 won-lost record, 0 saves,
4.50 ERA

He was immediately dubbed the "$2.3-Million Man," a nickname that Wayne Garland hated, especially after it eventually became a term of derision. It was coined after the Indians made Garland one of baseball's first millionaire free agents on November 19, 1976, shortly after the advent of free agency.

Garland was coming off a big season—a 20-7 record and 2.67 earned run average—with Baltimore, where he was paid $23,500. The Indians signed him to a 10-year, no cut, no trade, totally guaranteed contract worth $2.3-million. It was the largest, in both dollars and term, in the history of baseball at that time, and Garland himself said, retrospectively, "You guys [in the media] must have thought the Indians were idiots. I know a lot of people did."

The deal—a $300,000 signing bonus and annual salaries of $200,000—as well as the length of Garland's contract, stunned everybody, including Cleveland fans who'd grown weary of the Tribe being a perennial also-ran for more than two decades.

It also, at least at the onset, did exactly what Indian chiefs Alva (Ted) Bonda, principal owner of the franchise, and Phil Seghi, the general manager, had hoped.

"We wanted to prove we had money and would spend it for players who could help us win," Bonda said back then. (He died in 2005.)

Seghi, who died in 1987, stressed the importance of adding Garland to the Tribe pitching staff and also emphasized that the Indians were willing and able to pay whatever was necessary to improve the team. Since then, of course, baseball salaries have escalated wildly, so much so that in 2006 the major-league *minimum* salary was $327,000, nearly $100,000 more than Garland's *average* salary of $230,000.

Despite the high expectations of Bonda and Seghi, as well as the Cleveland fans—and, certainly, Garland, too—the Indians' gamble proved to be a financial disaster. It failed—not because Garland didn't try hard to justify the lavish contract, but probably because he tried *too* hard.

After a somewhat promising first year with the Indians in 1977, Garland suffered a rotator cuff injury the following spring training and underwent surgery on May 5, 1978, after which, he said, he came back too soon.

"It's usually a two-year process, one to get over the surgery, the second to rebuild strength. But, like a fool, 10 months later I pitched a game in spring training [1979] and my arm was never the same."

He had a second rotator cuff operation in 1989.

Later he also underwent five operations on his back for an injury the neurosurgeon said could be traced back to Garland's pitching career. As a result, he is now on total disability. "I can't do much of anything," he said. "I dabble a little in woodworking, but when I do, I hurt for the next two or three days.

"After my first back surgery [in 1995] the doctor told me I had the back of a 75-year-old man," said Garland, who was 45 at the time. "He probably was right. And now, when I'm on my feet for 15 or 20 minutes, my right leg goes numb and I have to sit down."

Garland lives in Las Vegas with his second wife, Kathie, whom he married in 1991. He had three children, daughter Ashley, and

*"You guys [in the media] must have
thought the Indians were idiots.
I know a lot of people did."*

———————————

sons Todd and Brett with his first wife Mary. They separated in an ugly divorce in 1987, after which Garland said, "I lost everything . . . house, a business, my car, everything."

On the surface, his first season with the Indians was nothing to rave about, although it showed some promise. Garland lost his first four decisions and didn't win a game until May 11. He was 7-9 at the All-Star break, and finished with a 13-19 record.

"I'm the first to admit it wasn't the kind of year everybody expected," he acknowledged. "But I think it was damned good. I pitched 21 complete games, and you don't pitch that many over the course of a season if you are not pitching well."

Unfortunately for Garland—and the Indians—his career began to unravel in 1978 when he hurt his arm pitching on a cold and windy day in a spring-training game.

"I felt a twinge in my shoulder on my very first pitch. I didn't think too much of it at the time and, like a fool, I kept pitching and eventually it got worse. I kept on pitching, though I don't think I was throwing 60 miles an hour, but I still wouldn't give in to it."

Finally, he had no choice. On April 29, against Oakland, Garland couldn't continue after the first couple of innings. "I called [coach] Dave Duncan to the mound and told him I couldn't get the ball to the plate, that something was very wrong."

It was. Six days later, following the rotator cuff operation, his season ended with a 2-3 record and a bloated 7.89 ERA.

Thereafter, upon his returning to the Tribe too soon in 1979, the remainder of Garland's career—shortened to five years—was miserable, personally and professionally.

His once congenial association with Seghi deteriorated, and his relationship with Gabe Paul, who had returned to the Indians in 1978 after five years with the New York Yankees, also became contentious.

"They didn't believe that my arm was as bad as it was," said Garland. "A lot of things happened that never came out [in the media]. They were always telling me, 'We're paying you a helluva lot of money and it's time you start earning it.'

"Once, when Gabe told me I wasn't worth the contract that Bonda and Seghi gave me, I told him, 'I never asked for it. They offered it to me. What do you want me to do? Give the money back?'

"Sometimes my arm felt pretty good, other times I couldn't lift it over my head without a lot of pain. It felt like I was trying to raise an anvil. But they wanted me to pitch. I tried but couldn't.

"I was told after the surgery that I'd have peaks and valleys, that my arm would be good one time, but not the next. They were right. One night in Baltimore I was throwing the ball pretty good, and then I made a pitch, felt a pop in my shoulder, and fell down to my knees in pain."

His ever-worsening relationship with Paul and Seghi and the ever-increasing taunting by the fans who had expected so much embittered Garland.

"Every time I pitched I was the '$2.3-Million Man,' not just Wayne Garland," he said. "Of course I didn't like it. I was sick of it. There also were times we'd have some work done at our house, like painting or paper hanging or something, and as soon as I told them my name, the price doubled.

"It seemed everyone resented the money the Indians offered," he said, with emphasis—again—on *offered.* "They held a grudge against me, and there was nothing I could do about it. It wasn't like I went out and hurt myself on purpose."

Garland was on and off the disabled list often in 1979, when he posted a 4-10 record in 18 games, and in 1980 when he was 6-9, and 3-7 in 1981.

After the 1981 season ended, the Indians bit the bullet and released Garland with five years remaining on his guaranteed contract for a total of one million dollars. It ended Garland's nine-year major-league pitching career with a 55-66 record and 3.89 ERA in 190 games. His record with the Indians was 28-48 with a 4.50 ERA in 99 appearances.

If he had it to do all over again, Garland said, not entirely facetiously, "I'd win 20 games every one of those 10 years in my contract with the Indians, I wouldn't hurt my arm, and then I'd walk away. Otherwise, there's nothing I'd change."

Then, to clarify any possible misunderstanding, he said, "I have no animosity toward anyone. You guys [in the media] were only doing your job. And the fans . . . well, they were just tired of losing. I don't blame them."

As a parting comment, Garland said, "I'd like people to remember I was the guy who chose to play for the Indians back when nobody wanted to play in Cleveland. Now everybody does.

"And, sure, they paid me what was big money then, but remember, I didn't ask for it, they offered it. And who wouldn't have taken it?"

TITO
FRANCONA

Outfielder, First Baseman, 1959–64

Best season: 1959, 122 games, .363 batting average, 20 home runs, 79 RBI

Indians career: 000 games, .000 avg., 00 home runs, 00 RBI

There were many what-ifs in Tito Francona's 15-season major-league career, two of which stand out in particular:

What if Jimmy Piersall had not complained to Indians manager Joe Gordon that, because of the late-afternoon sun, he didn't feel comfortable playing center field in the second game of a double header against New York at Cleveland Stadium on June 7, 1959?

And what if Francona's left leg had not been so severely injured that he was unable to play five games in late September that season, after the Indians were mathematically eliminated from the pennant race?

"When Piersall had a problem because of the sun, Gordon put me in center field," said Francona, who'd filled in at first base for slumping Vic Power and singled and homered in the opener. "From that game through the rest of the season everything seemed to click for me."

Indeed it did. Thereafter, Francona—who'd been acquired by the Tribe two weeks before the start of the season—was a regular in the lineup that season, either in the outfield, for 64 games, or first base, for 35 games.

*"I felt like I had a god on my shoulder every time
I went to the plate. There was no way a pitcher
could throw a ball past me. Not that season."*

And, in contrast, "When my leg was so bad late in the season [trainer] Wally Bock warned me that I could cause serious damage if I continued to play, and insisted that I rest it for a few games," added Francona.

If Francona had not established himself as a regular in the lineup at either center field or first base, he would not have had the opportunity to come this close to winning the 1959 American League batting championship. And if he had not been forced out of the lineup when the torn hamstring muscle caused his leg to turn black, it's probable Francona would have batted enough times to qualify for the title that was won by Harvey Kuenn, his former teammate with the Tigers.

Francona hit for a .363 average (145 hits in 399 official times at-bat), 10 percentage points higher than Kuenn's .353 (198-for-561). But he didn't have enough *total* plate appearances to qualify for the championship. The rule then in effect required a player to make at least 477 total plate appearances—which included walks, sacrifices, and times hit by pitches.

In 1959, Francona walked 35 times, was credited with six sacrifices, and reached base as a hit batsman on three occasions for 443 total plate appearances, 34 short of the amount specified in the rule. Thus, Francona would have needed to play eight or nine more games to reach the minimum requirement—and the way things were "clicking" for him that season, it's safe to assume he would have made enough hits to hold his lead over Kuenn.

As Francona said from his home in New Brighton, Pennsylvania, "I felt like I had a god on my shoulder every time I went to the plate. There was no way a pitcher could throw a ball past me. No way. Not anybody. Not that season." Which must have been true because, as late as August 10 he was batting over .400.

Francona's sore hamstring, and a similar injury suffered by teammate Chuck Tanner, also factored in his failed bid for the title.

"There were times I got screwed out of hits because, after I'd hurt my leg, I couldn't run full speed and couldn't beat out balls that normally would have been hits."

On at least one occasion, "Tanner could hardly run because of a bad leg and was forced at second by the right fielder—the *right fielder!*—when I hit a line shot that would have been a hit if nobody had been on base," he said.

In the years since his final game, with the Brewers on September 29, 1970, the former outfielder/first baseman—and almost-batting champion—has had two open-heart surgeries, in 1992 and 2001, and both knees replaced at the same time in 2005.

As he suggested, fans who might remember him from the years he played in Cleveland probably would be surprised to see him now. "My height has increased by two or three inches, that's how bad my legs were bowed. My wife, Jean, calls me 'Betty Grable' because my legs look so much better now."

Francona lost his first wife, Roberta, to cancer in 1992. She was the mother of their two children, daughter Amy and son Terry, who played 10 years in the major leagues, including 1988 with the Indians. Terry managed the Philadelphia Phillies from 1997 to 2000 and took over as manager of the Boston Red Sox in 2004.

Terry was born on April 22, 1959, which was 42 days before his dad replaced Piersall in center field for the Indians, launching his near-batting championship season. And now, of course, it's Terry and the Red Sox who command most of Francona's attention.

"People asked me if I coached him when he was a kid, which I didn't because I never had time, I was always playing. And when Boston won the World Series [in 2004] they asked me if I give him [managerial] advice, which of course I don't," he said.

When he signed as a 19-year-old amateur with the St. Louis

Browns in 1952, Francona received a $10,000 bonus. He was in the army in 1954 and 1955, reached the major leagues with Baltimore in 1956, spent 1958 with the Chicago White Sox and Detroit, and was traded to the Indians on March 21, 1959.

That first year with the Tribe his salary was $10,000; it doubled to $20,000 in 1960. The most he ever made in baseball, Francona said, was $29,500 in 1962, after a brief holdout with Indian chief Gabe Paul. "I liked Gabe, but oh! was he tough to deal with. In those days players had no choice because management had all the power."

As for agents, Francona chuckled and said, "There was no such thing in my day. If you brought in an agent, they [the owners] would throw you out."

It is ironic that on two occasions Francona was traded in deals involving Larry Doby. The first was in 1958, when the Orioles sent Francona to the Chicago White Sox, and the second in 1959, when the Tigers dealt Doby even-up for Francona. It also was ironic that, the season following their classic battle for the batting championship, Francona and Kuenn wound up as teammates—and as roommates on the road—after the Indians acquired Kuenn in Frank Lane's infamous trade for Rocky Colavito.

Francona said they never talked about Kuenn winning the batting championship, or that he won it because Francona did not have enough at-bats. "It never really dawned on me how good it would have been if I had won. In fact, I never thought much about it until you guys [in the media] asked about the what-ifs."

Francona played for nine teams in his major-league career: St. Louis Cardinals, Philadelphia Phillies, Atlanta, Oakland, Milwaukee Brewers, Orioles, White Sox, Tigers, and Indians.

"I never played on a pennant winner," he said. "I always seemed to be one year too late or one year too early."

Thus, "When Terry and the Red Sox won [the World Series in 2004], it was almost as great a thrill for me as it was for him. Before that I hardly ever watched a World Series game on television . . . I was always too jealous of the guys who were in it," said Francona.

The closest Francona came to playing in a World Series was 1959, when the Indians collapsed in the final two weeks and finished second, five games behind the White Sox.

"We could have won it; OK, maybe we *should* have won it," Francona said about the Indians' failed bid to win the pennant in 1959. "We had the best team."

Just as some would say about Francona's failed bid for the batting championship in 1959: that he could have won it; OK, perhaps even that he *should* have won it.

DICK
BOSMAN

Pitcher, 1973–75

Best season: 1974, 25 games,
7-5 won-lost record, 0 saves,
4.10 ERA

Indians career: 53 games,
8-15 won-lost record, 0 saves,
34.91 ERA

When he came to Cleveland in 1973, after the Indians acquired him from Texas, Dick Bosman was not a happy man. "For one thing, I wanted to stay with the Rangers. I grew up with the [Washington/ Texas] organization and I didn't want to leave.

"For another thing, I also didn't want to go to Cleveland, which, in those days, was not considered a good place to play," he also made clear.

But, strange as it seems, he was even unhappier two years later upon *leaving* Cleveland when the Tribe dealt him to Oakland, even though his new team had won the American League pennant each of the previous three seasons.

"I changed my mind [about the Indians] because of the way I was made to feel welcome by the fans and the media, and especially by [trainer] Jimmy Warfield, Buddy Bell, Gaylord Perry, Jack Brohamer, and John Lowenstein, among others," said Bosman.

"I thank God for those who had such an impact on me and my career, including [manager] Kenny Aspromonte. He fought for me when Phil Seghi wanted to get rid of me, which he finally did after he fired Aspromonte," said Bosman, who makes his home in Palm

Harbor, Florida, with his wife Pam, whom he married in 1969, and their three children.

It was during his time with the Tribe that Bosman reached the pinnacle of his career, on July 19, 1974, with a no-hitter that—except for his own error—would have been only the eighth perfect game in the history of baseball at that time.

It was against Oakland, and his 4-0 near-masterpiece in the old Cleveland Municipal Stadium might have been what convinced the A's flamboyant owner, Charley Finley, to trade for Bosman.

Bosman recalled the miscue that cost him a perfect game. It happened in the fourth inning when Sal Bando nubbed a bounder to the third base side of the pitcher's mound.

"It's an easy play . . . I've made it hundreds of times. You take a couple of steps to your right, pick up the ball, and just sort of flip it to first base."

But that time it wasn't automatic. Bosman grabbed the ball and flipped it to first baseman Tom McCraw.

Except he threw the ball over McCraw's head.

"I'm sorry I screwed it up but, hey, it was only the fourth inning and at that point nobody was thinking about a no-hitter, let alone a perfect game. I surely wasn't."

It was the only no-hitter of Bosman's career, though he came close two other times when he pitched for Washington. The first was in 1969 in a game against the Indians, when Tony Horton got the only hit, a broken-bat single. And in 1970, Minnesota's Cesar Tovar led off the game with a bunt single, but Bosman retired all but one of the next 27 batters around a sixth inning walk to opposing pitcher Jim Kaat.

Bosman was signed by Pittsburgh as an amateur free agent in 1963, later that season was claimed by San Francisco in the minor-league draft, and in November 1964 was acquired in a minor-league deal by the Washington Senators. He pitched his first major-league game on June 1, 1966.

In his 11-year major-league career, Bosman compiled an 82-85 won-lost record with a 3.67 earned run average. In 1969, when he was 14-5 for the Senators, his 2.19 ERA was the best in the American League.

The Senators (who became the Texas Rangers in 1972) traded Bosman, with outfielder Ted Ford, to the Indians for pitcher Steve Dunning on May 10, 1973.

Two years and ten days later, on May 20, 1975, the Indians (*read: Phil Seghi*) sent Bosman with another pitcher, Jim Perry, to the A's for pitcher Blue Moon Odom. As usual back then, the Indians also received money in the deal, reportedly $50,000.

Bosman retired after the 1976 season, when he earned his peak major-league salary, $54,000, about which he said, "I had to fight like crazy to get a $2,000 raise."

Admittedly disenchanted with Finley, Bosman reluctantly gave up the game he loved, though only temporarily. For the next nine years he worked with a friend at a car dealership in the Washington area and coached young players as they progressed through Little League, Babe Ruth League, high school, and American Legion baseball.

"I found out I enjoyed working with kids and that I was good at it. In effect I was serving an apprenticeship, learning how to coach, which was something I had never aspired to do," he said.

Thus when Alvin Dark, his former manager with the A's, became farm director of the Chicago White Sox in 1986, Bosman was offered a job as a minor league coach.

"I wasn't sure I wanted to do it, after being home for nine years, but my wife talked me into it." Pam did so in a not-so-subtle way, he said. "'Go ahead and do it . . . you know you're a better coach than you were a player,' she told me, so I went back, and the rest is history."

Bosman finished the season as pitching coach of the White Sox and stayed with them through 1987, then coached for Baltimore at its Class AAA Rochester team from 1988 to 1991, was promoted to the Orioles under manager Johnny Oates in 1992, and from 1993 to 2000 coached for Oates with Texas.

"'Go ahead and do it . . . you know you're a better coach than you were a player,' she told me."

"We [Rangers] won the division in 1998 and 1999 but couldn't get past the Yankees in the playoffs either year. When we didn't get it done [win the pennant] in 2000 . . . well, you can't fire the whole staff, so you let the pitching coach go," said Bosman, who had one year left on his contract.

He went home to the Washington area where he owned an automobile body shop and built hot rods. Soon there came an offer from the Tampa Bay Devil Rays to return to baseball in 2001, this time as a teacher/coach in the low minor leagues.

"They told me they wanted a veteran to work with their young kids, to get them started on the right foot. I wasn't sure I wanted to do it. I wasn't bitter, I was just burned out," he said.

"Pam and I talked about it again. I told her I needed a sign. We prayed about it and I got my answer. Suddenly I could see myself coaching those young kids."

Bosman went to Tampa Bay's lowest-rung minor league team, Hudson Valley (in Poughkeepsie, New York) of the New York-Penn rookie league. "It rejuvenated me," he said. For the next three seasons (2002–2004) he coached at the Class AA level, then returned in 2005 to "teach the kids" at Hudson Valley.

"I'm doing something I've come to love, in a game I've always loved," said Bosman. The New York-Penn League consists of only 70 games, doesn't start until June, and is finished in September, so he's able to be home with Pam and their two adopted children almost nine months of the year.

"I'm grateful for what I have, and I'm grateful for the help I received along the way, from people like Aspromonte and, later, Ted Williams," who was Bosman's manager with Washington and Texas from 1969 to 1972.

"I had a marvelous relationship with Williams, who probably was the greatest hitter in the history of baseball, and because he was such a great hitter, he also knew so much about pitching.

"Most of the things I benefited from as a pitcher, and that I teach the kids I coach, came from Williams, from the neck up. I had pretty good stuff when I was with the Senators, I just didn't have an idea how to use it. Until one day in spring training [1969] with Williams. We had a private moment together, and he said to me, 'You have a chance to be pretty good, but you have to learn how to use what you've got.'

"I said, 'OK, when do we start?' and he said, 'We just did.' From then on I was like a disciple at his feet. I was taught by others the physical part of how to deliver a baseball, but Ted is the one who taught me the when and how part of pitching.

"Which is what I'm trying to do now with the kids I'm coaching."

STEVE
DUNNING

Pitcher, 1970–74

Best season: 1971, 31 games,
8-14 won-lost record, 0 saves,
4.50 ERA

Indians career: 70 games,
18-29 won-lost record, 1 save,
4.37 ERA

It didn't take long for the sportswriters in Cleveland to begin calling him "Stunning Steve" Dunning after he was selected in the first round (second overall) of the 1970 amateur draft.

Eleven days later, on June 14, the 21-year-old Dunning—one of the first players to go directly from college to the major leagues— pitched and won his first start in professional baseball.

It had a nice ring to it, did "Stunning Steve," similar as it was to "Sudden Sam," the nickname bestowed upon Sam McDowell, who also was a member of the Indians back then.

Fresh out of Stanford University, Dunning struck out the first batter he faced in his professional baseball debut, and was the winning pitcher as the Indians beat Milwaukee, 9-2.

"I admit thinking to myself, 'This isn't so tough,'" he said about pitching in the major leagues. "I guess I figured it always would be the way it was that day."

Actually, it seemed to get even better for Dunning the following season. On Opening Day, April 18, 1971, he hurled a one-hitter against the Washington Senators. After the game their manager, Hall of Famer Ted Williams, flat-out predicted that Dunning would

*"I admit thinking to myself,
'This isn't so tough.' I guess I figured
it always would be the way it was."*

be "some kind of pitcher someday." Unfortunately, that "someday" never arrived for Dunning, as Williams's lavish praise proved premature. So did the pitcher's nickname.

By mid-1978 the hard-throwing right-hander was out of baseball after compiling a 23-41 major-league career record over seven seasons, many parts of which he spent in the minor leagues with six organizations, in addition to the Indians.

Dunning was traded to Texas on May 10, 1973, and subsequently wore the uniforms of the Chicago White Sox, California Angels, Montreal Expos, St. Louis Cardinals, Oakland Athletics, and San Diego Padres. It finally ended for Dunning on July 1, 1978, at Class AAA Hawaii, a Padres farm club.

He said, "I pitched a complete game shutout, went into the manager's office, and told him I was quitting baseball, that I was going to law school," which he did, a month later.

"It really wasn't a difficult decision. I was 29 years old, and nobody back in those days gave a 29-year-old pitcher a chance to start over."

From his office in Irvine, California, Dunning insisted he feels no remorse about the brevity of his baseball career, or even its eventual demise.

"I have absolutely no regrets. I can't complain about anything. I am doing great. Life is good. I was fortunate to go back to law school and find something I really enjoy, not as much as I enjoyed playing baseball, but almost as much."

He has been practicing law since 1981 as a partner in the firm of Higham, McConnell, and Dunning.

Dunning's wife, Kim, who wrote a column on the sports page of the *Plain Dealer* when he pitched for the Tribe, also earned a law degree and has been a judge in the Superior Court in Orange County since 1997. Kim and Steve were classmates at Stanford University, graduated together in 1970, and were married three months later. Then, heading off the obvious question about a possible conflict, Dunning chuckled and said, "There's no problem. Kim handles contract disputes in civil cases, and I am a transaction lawyer. I deal with real estate and securities matters, but no litigation. I never go to court. I wouldn't know what to do if I had to go to court."

They have one son, Justin, born in 1977. He also graduated from Stanford and was a pitcher. Seattle picked Justin in the 12th round of the 1998 amateur draft, and he later was traded to the New York Mets and subsequently to Los Angeles. Justin reached the Class AA level before giving up his baseball career in 2003 to return to the Sports Management graduate program at Arizona State.

Among Steve's fondest memories, of course, was that first major-league game when the 25,380 fans in attendance in the old Cleveland Municipal Stadium helped the Indians pay the $60,000 signing bonus they gave him.

After he struck out Tommy Harper to open the game, Dunning went on to pitch five innings, leaving with a 5-2 lead on a yield of five hits and two walks, with three strikeouts.

"It was unbelievable, overwhelming to be given the opportunity to pitch in the big leagues immediately, and to win to boot," Dunning said of his spectacular debut. "It was almost beyond comprehension. I'd wanted to be a major-league baseball player my whole life, so it was a dream come true. It doesn't come any better than that."

Actually, it almost did for Dunning—a near no-hitter against Washington in the 1971 opener. It was spoiled early, in the second inning by Tom McCraw, who would become Dunning's teammate the following season.

During his three-plus seasons with the Tribe, Dunning's overall record was 18-29. "I threw in the high 90s [mph], though they didn't have those sophisticated radar guns they have now," he said. "Back then it was Sam McDowell and me. They said I was the second hardest thrower in the league."

While his fastball might have been second only to McDowell's, Dunning admits, "My career was limited because I never had an effective breaking pitch. And to be successful as a starter, you need something in addition to a fastball. I was a one-pitch pitcher most of my career.

"If I were playing today, somebody probably would make me a reliever. You can be successful out of the bullpen with one pitch. But when you have to face batters three or four times a game, you better have something else to show them, I don't care how hard you throw.

"Once I came to that realization, it was time for me to go [retire], which I did—and I don't have any regrets," he said again. "Believe me. I had my shot. I had my 15 minutes of fame, but I just wasn't good enough. I was a journeyman pitcher at best.

"If I had stayed in baseball another five years I would now be five years behind my career in law. I am making . . . oh, probably twenty times more [money] practicing law than my highest salary in baseball," which was $35,000 with the Indians in 1972.

In addition to his stunning debut in 1970 and near no-hitter in 1971, it also was Dunning's bat for which he will be remembered as long as the American League retains the designated hitter rule. He was the last A.L. pitcher to hit a grand slam home run, against Oakland at the old Stadium on May 11, 1971.

"It's been more than thirty years, but I can still see it," he said of the homer. "The count was 3-and-2 and Diego Segui threw me a fastball, up and over the plate. I swung and hit it over the left center field fence. The only bad thing was that we didn't win the game."

Dunning hit three home runs in 1972, when his pitching record was 6-4 and his batting average was .273. "I basically won four of my own games," he said.

"Pitching for the Indians in those days was somewhat frustrating. We were a young ball club, and most of the time we were all developing together. I was learning and so was everybody else. We didn't have any superstars. Oh, we got Ken Harrelson, but he got hurt. Tony Horton was good, but he had emotional problems. And Ray Fosse was having a great year in 1970 but then got hurt in the All-Star Game and was never the same.

"It was one frustration after another. You can look at all the things that happened to us and say, 'I wonder what if . . .'

"I regret that we didn't do better back then, and I wish my career had been as 'stunning' as you guys [in the media] thought it might be. But that's all. And everything has turned out for the best, for me, believe me."

DOC
EDWARDS

Catcher, Coach, Manager, 1962–63,
1985–87, 1987–89

Best season: 1962, 53 games,
.273 batting average, 3 home runs,
9 RBI

Indians career: 63 games,
.270 avg., 3 home runs, 9 RBI

Howard Edwards, best known as "Doc," was a member of the U.S. Navy Medical Corps prior to being signed as an amateur free agent by the Indians in 1958. He had an unspectacular major-league playing career which, he admits, "is putting it mildly."

And though Edwards didn't distinguish himself as a hitter, he caught for the Tribe, Kansas City Athletics, New York Yankees, and Philadelphia from 1962 to 1965 and 1970, and is among the few who have done "just about everything" in the game.

"Name it, I did it," he says, and is still doing it in his fifth decade as a baseball lifer, after starting in the game at the age of 21.

And despite his brief tenure in Cleveland as a player, as well as a coach and manager, Edwards insists, "My heart was, still is, and always will be with the Indians," which, it seems, is a good enough reason to include him in this book.

At last report Edwards was serving as director of player personnel for the Sioux Falls Canaries in the independent Northern League. It's a team operated by Mike Veeck, son of the late Bill Veeck, who owned the Indians in 1948, the last time they won the World Series. Until 2005 Edwards also was manager of the Canaries.

Doc caught in the minor leagues for four seasons, was promoted to the Indians in 1962, was traded (along with $100,000 cash) to Kansas City in May 1963 in the deal that brought catcher Joe Azcue and shortstop Dick Howser to Cleveland, and went on to play through 1965 in the major leagues, then back in the minors through 1969, and with the Phillies as a player-coach in 1970, when he retired at the age of 34.

But Edwards wasn't gone long from baseball. He went on to coach in the minors for the Yankees, and then managed for 13 years in the Baltimore, Chicago Cubs, Montreal, and Indians farm systems. He became the Tribe's bullpen coach in 1985, replaced Pat Corrales as manager on July 16, 1987, and was fired on September 12, 1989, when John Hart, then a Tribe scout, took over as interim manager. Shortly thereafter Edwards committed "the one mistake in my baseball life," he said.

"Oh, I screwed up a lot, but they were just little things. That one stupid mistake was when [general manager] Hank Peters offered me a job as his assistant after he let me go as manager. Hank told me that nobody in the organization, except himself, would have more to say than me, and that he was sure I could handle the responsibility.

"But, foolishly, I listened to my wife at the time because a bench [coach's] job with the Mets came up that paid more money. So I took the money instead of staying with the Indians, where my heart was, still is, and always will be.

"I didn't realize how important the job, as assistant to the general manager, would be. I really feel that if I had taken the job that Hank offered, I would still be associated with the Indians."

Then, for emphasis, Edwards added, "I'm a country boy from Red Jacket, West Virginia, but I will be an Indian until the day I die, no matter where I am or what I may be doing."

Edwards's managerial career with the Indians was as unspectacular as his playing career, though the organization at that time had few good players as it was evolving through the financially unstable ownership of the estate of the late F. J. "Steve" O'Neill.

Richard Jacobs and his brother, David, purchased the franchise in December of 1986 but had not yet loosened the purse strings that would transform the Indians into the winning team they became in the 1990s.

"I don't want to put the knock on anybody," Edwards said of his two-plus seasons at the helm of the Indians, during which they won 173 games and lost 207, finishing seventh in 1987 and sixth in both 1988 and 1989.

"We had some decent players, but not enough of them. We were always a little short and we couldn't—or wouldn't—go out and get the help we needed."

It was the closest Edwards came to criticizing the front office's apparent unwillingness or inability to buy or deal for players to improve the team.

Actually, the Indians under Edwards in 1988 played very well the first half of the season and were in first place or challenging for the lead until late June, when they were 39-29—only two games behind the leader. But then the bottom dropped out. Their record slipped to 45-43 at the All-Star break; they fell to 52-53 by the end of July and never climbed back to .500 the rest of the season.

"When it [the season] started, everyone in the organization was in agreement that it would be a building year," said Edwards. "But then, when we were going so good, everybody got excited and thought we had a chance to win [the pennant]—and we did have a chance, but not without some help."

But help wasn't forthcoming. And, when the season ended, the Indians were eight games under .500 at 78-84, and 11 games out of first place. Edwards's demise as manager came after 143 games—65 victories, 78 losses—in 1989. Ironically, Hart, who took over the team when Edwards was fired, became Peters's assistant in 1990, the job that Edwards said he'd been offered a year earlier.

When he played for the Indians in 1962 and part of 1963, Edwards was assigned by general manager Gabe Paul to be Sam McDowell's roommate. It was a plan designed by Paul for Edwards to keep McDowell out of trouble. They had played together the previous season at Class AAA Salt Lake City.

"Sam was only 19 or 20 back then, and was as pure as the driven snow," said Edwards. So, what happened to McDowell, who admittedly drank himself out of baseball? "I don't know," answered Edwards. "What I do know is that Sam had the best four pitches—fastball, curve, slider and change-up—of anybody I ever caught."

Edwards, his second wife, Connie, whom he married in 1981, and their son Eric make their home in Vero Beach, Florida. He and his first wife had four children, Shirley, Mickey, Jim, and Michelle.

Edwards survived a near-fatal heart attack and underwent quadruple bypass surgery when he managed Class AAA Buffalo in 1992. "I was at home, at that time in Humphrey, New York, and that's when my faith in God really got deep," he said.

"It was miracle, because just two weeks previously one of my sons moved into a house that I owned nearby, and two days before I had the heart attack I programmed my phone for one-button dialing. If I hadn't done that, I am sure I would have died because, when the heart attack hit, I could only push one button on the phone, and it was for my son. He came and got me to the hospital in Olean [New York] in time.

"I will always remember . . . if I hadn't programmed my telephone when I did, I would not have been able to call for help, so I'm grateful . . . grateful to my son, the doctor who operated on me, and, of course, to God."

And so, Edwards continues his love affair and life in baseball. "I'll be somewhere in the game until I die, you can be sure of that," he said. "My only regret is that one stupid mistake I made a long time ago. But then, who would have ever thought that this old country boy would ever get to manage the Cleveland Indians?

"It was a great part of my life, though I wish it could have lasted longer."

LARRY
BROWN

Shortstop, Second Baseman, Third Baseman, 1963–71

Best season: 1965, 124 games, .253 batting average, 8 home runs, 40 RBI

Indians career: 941 games, .238 avg., 45 home runs, 231 RBI

Forty-six years after Indians shortstop Ray Chapman became the only major-league baseball player killed in a game, history almost repeated itself.

Chapman suffered a fractured skull and died on August 17, 1920, while playing against the New York Yankees. On May 4, 1966, also in a game against the Yankees, another Indians shortstop, Larry Brown, came close to death when he was involved in a horrific collision with a teammate.

"I don't remember what happened . . . all I know is that I was told that [trainer] Wally Bock saved my life," said Brown from his home in Wellington, Florida.

Bock did so by forcing open Brown's mouth to prevent him from swallowing his tongue, which would have choked the 26-year-old shortstop.

The collision occurred as Brown was racing into short left field near the foul line, trying to catch a pop fly hit by Roger Maris in Yankee Stadium. He collided with outfielder Leon Wagner, and both players were knocked unconscious.

Brown was rushed to Lenox Hill Hospital in New York, where he remained in a coma for three days. Later he was transferred to a hospital in Cleveland.

Brown's injuries were extensive: multiple fractures of the skull (above and below his eyes) and a broken nose, and he was hemorrhaging from every cavity in his head. Initially it was feared he suffered brain damage, though subsequent neurological tests were negative. Surgery was required to repair damage to a muscle in his left eye.

The collision happened in the fourth inning of a game the Indians won, 2-1, behind pitcher Sonny Siebert, on a ninth-inning home run by Fred Whitfield.

Wagner escaped with only a broken nose and played the next night, causing Brown to quip, "Don't tell me that all men are created equal." Brown's face was so battered and swollen that his wife, Helen, who flew to New York the next day, couldn't find him in the hospital's intensive care unit—because she didn't recognize him—and had to be directed by a nurse to his bedside.

All told, Brown was hospitalized 18 days, 10 in New York and 8 in Cleveland. Incredibly, he returned to play only 43 days after the near-fatal collision. And, as fate would have it, Brown's first game back also was at Yankee Stadium, on June 16, a game that, unlike the one on May 4, Brown vividly remembers.

"I got a standing ovation from the New York fans when my name was announced in the starting lineup," said Brown. "It probably was the only standing ovation I ever got, and it is one of the great memories of my career."

Though Brown knows the details of his near-fatal accident with Wagner only as they were related to him by teammates and the media, he easily recalled a "true" highlight of his 12-year major-league career. He played nine seasons with the Tribe (1963–71) and later for Oakland, Baltimore, and Texas through 1974.

The game Brown likes to recall was the nightcap of a double header on July 31, 1963, a 9-5 victory over the Los Angeles Angels at Cleveland's old Municipal Stadium. "How could I not remember it . . . and how could I not like it?" asked Brown. It took place a few weeks after he was promoted from the minor leagues.

Four members of the Indians—the fourth of whom was Brown— hit consecutive home runs against Angels' right-hander Paul Foytack. First it was Woodie Held, followed by Pedro Ramos, and then Tito Francona.

As Brown stepped into the batter's box, "I expected to get knocked down, no doubt about it, and I kind of eased back on my heels on Foytack's first pitch," he said. "But the ball was over the plate for a called strike. Same thing on the second pitch.

"Now I'm thinking, 'He's got two strikes on me . . . I'm going down for sure.' But again Foytack's next pitch was right down the middle. I swung and hit the ball out." It was Brown's first major-league home run.

Only moments after the ball landed among the left field seats. Angels manager Bill Rigney called in a relief pitcher. "It wasn't because Foytack gave up four consecutive home runs . . . it was because *I* hit one of them," joked Brown. He went on to hit 47 homers with a career batting average of .233 in 1,129 major-league games.

It started, he said, "Because I was in the right place at the right time."

The Indians gave him a $6,500 bonus to sign as an amateur free agent in 1958. At the time Larry's older brother Dick was a catcher for the Indians (1957–59). Dick later played for the Chicago White Sox (1960), Detroit (1961–62), and Baltimore (1963–65); he died of a brain tumor in 1970.

After five-plus seasons in the minors as an outstanding defensive middle infielder, Brown was promoted to Cleveland on July 6, 1963. He was called up after injuries sidelined Dick Howser, the Tribe's regular shortstop, and Woodie Held, an outfielder-shortstop.

It was to be only a temporary promotion, but Brown made it permanent. "I got some hits and made some plays [at shortstop and second base] and all of a sudden [manager] Birdie Tebbetts decided he wanted to see more of me."

"There were a lot of times I wished I had stayed in baseball, but not anymore. The game has changed too much, especially the players."

Many years later, after both men had retired, they met at an old-timers' game. Brown said, "I thanked Birdie for giving me a chance, and he said, 'Don't thank me, Brownie. You were the best damned shortstop in the American League when you played for me,' which was one of the nicest things anyone ever said to me."

Brown and his wife, Leni, whom he married in 1962, have three daughters, Laurie, born in 1963, Leslie, 1964, and Leigh, 1967.

Brown, who won the Indians "Good Guy" award in 1970, said of his baseball career, "I loved playing in Cleveland. The fans were great. They're knowledgeable . . . they know the guys who bust their butts, and they always treated me well, respectfully. We weren't very good back then, and our season was usually over in June, but we had some good times, especially 1966, except when I got hurt that season.

"That's one time I was in the wrong place at the right time, or the right place at the wrong time," Brown said, referring to his collision with Wagner.

The Indians started the 1966 season with 10 consecutive victories, and 13 in their first 14 games. But they finished fifth in the 10-team American League, 17 games out of first place. Tebbetts was fired on August 19, six weeks before the season ended.

Brown's top salary with the Indians was $26,000 in 1969, and $30,000 in each of his last three years when he played for the Athletics, Orioles, and Rangers.

"There were a lot of times I wished I had stayed in baseball, but not anymore," he said. "The game has changed too much, especially the players. I don't know how much respect they have for their managers and coaches, the way things are now.

"I hope the players appreciate what they've got going for themselves, with the money they're making and everything. Sure, you have to wonder how much longer it can go on, but the owners are smart enough, and if they couldn't afford to pay the players what they do, they probably wouldn't be doing it."

And finally, on the subject of steroids, Brown was particularly outspoken.

"Whatever is happening, baseball let it happen, and I think [commissioner] Bud Selig is a disgrace. It's hard for me to believe that he and others [owners] didn't know what was going on. They must have been hiding their heads in the sand—or they didn't want to know what was happening.

"If [the use of steroids] is out of control, it's because they let it happen, and now they've got to pay the price to correct it."

DUANE
KUIPER

Second Baseman, 1974–81

Best season: 1978, 149 games, .283 batting average, 0 home runs, 43 RBI

Indians career: 786 games, .274 avg., 1 home run, 221 RBI

It is entirely possible, though difficult to verify, that Duane Kuiper, a.k.a. "Captain Kuip" when he played for the Indians, has personally seen and called over the air more of Barry Bonds's home runs than anyone.

By his own estimation, Kuiper, one of the radio and television voices of the San Francisco Giants—who was something of a home-run hitter himself—has "had the privilege of calling more than five hundred" of Bonds's homers. And in his role as a Giants broadcaster since Bonds arrived in San Francisco in 1993, Kuiper has developed great respect for the outfielder who has passed Babe Ruth and is second to only Hank Aaron as baseball's most prolific home-run hitter.

"I think [Bonds] will go down in history as the greatest hitter ever," said Kuiper, the Indians second baseman from 1974 to 1981 who was traded to the Giants and played for them into the 1985 season.

Kuiper has done play-by-play and color commentary on radio and/or television of Giants games since 1987, with the exception of one year, 1993, when he went to Denver as a radio voice of the Colorado Rockies.

Two younger brothers, Glen Kuiper and Jeff Kuiper, also are in broadcasting in the Bay Area, Glen as the television play-by-play announcer for the Oakland Athletics and Jeff as the producer for the station that carries the Giants games described by Duane. All three Kuipers have won numerous Northern California Emmy awards.

When asked his opinion of the ongoing and persistent speculation regarding Bonds's use of performance-enhancing drugs—i.e., steroids—Duane Kuiper carefully steered clear of expressing any comment that might be construed as incriminating.

"I don't know what's going to happen," he said, "but I do know that no one takes better care of himself than Barry Bonds. And when he says that he was not aware that the substance he was taking . . . that he was unaware of it [being a steroid or illegal substance] . . . until I know different, I am not going to doubt it.

"I have enough faith in him [that] if he looks me in the eyes, as he has done, and says, 'I am clean,' then I believe him."

Calling his broadcasting job "the second best in baseball . . . second only to playing in the major leagues," Kuiper covers 110 to 115 Giants games on television in San Francisco, as well as 40 to 50 on radio. He and his longtime broadcast partner, former major-league pitcher Mike Krukow, recently signed five-year contract extensions through 2010.

Kuiper's broadcasting career actually began in the late-1970s when he was still playing for the Indians. He did a daily five-minute commentary on radio station WELW in Willoughby, Ohio, that paid him $10 a show.

And, several years ago, after he'd established himself as one of the best broadcasters in baseball, Kuiper said he had "some very serious discussions" about possibly returning to Cleveland when Herb Score retired as a radio voice of the Indians.

At the time Kuiper also had some serious discussions with his wife, Michelle, and their two children about possibly leaving San Francisco. As he said, "I loved my [playing] career in Cleveland, the fans, the ball club, even you guys in the media, but I was outvoted, three to one."

The earlier reference to Kuiper being "something of a home-run hitter himself" was, obviously, sarcasm. As most fans know, the former second baseman hit one home run in his 12-year major-league career.

It was on August 29, 1977, in Kuiper's 1,382nd at-bat, against Steve Stone of the Chicago White Sox in a nationally televised game at Cleveland's old Municipal Stadium. The ball flew into the lower right field stands, and when Kuiper came around third base heading for home, "all the guys were at the plate to greet me," he said. "It was like I'd just hit a playoff game-winner." Thereafter, in his next 1,997 official at-bats through the end of his playing career, Kuiper didn't hit another homer, which he claimed—facetiously, of course—was intentional.

"One [home run] is better than none, but any more than that and people start expecting them," quipped Kuiper, who compiled a .271 career batting average in 1,057 games over eight seasons with the Indians, and three-plus with the Giants from 1982 to 1985.

Though his homer off Stone was the only one of his career, Kuiper did hit 29 triples, including two—both with the bases loaded—in one game against the New York Yankees on July 27, 1978. It tied a major-league record shared by two other players, Elmer Valo of Philadelphia in 1949, and Billy Bruton of Milwaukee in 1959.

Kuiper also has the distinction of having spoiled three potential no-hitters, and for having played in two no-hitters by Indians pitchers Dennis Eckersley (1977) and Lenny Barker (during his perfect game, 1981).

In the Eckersley no-hitter, won by the Tribe, 1-0, over the California Angels, Kuiper scored the game's only run after he tripled in the first inning and came home on a squeeze bunt by Jim Norris.

In his role as spoiler, Kuiper got the only hit in what would have been no-hitters by Andy Hassler of the Kansas City Royals in 1977, Nolan Ryan of the California Angels in 1978, and Ron Guidry of the

"When I went to San Francisco, I left my heart in Cleveland."

Yankees in 1978. Guidry, in his victory, gave up two hits, both by Kuiper.

The Indians' Man of the Year in 1977 and also winner of the Cleveland Baseball Writers Good Guy Award in 1978, Kuiper was one of the best fielding second basemen in baseball. He committed only nine errors in 1976, which led the American League, and nine again in 1979, when his .988 fielding percentage was the best in both major leagues.

A severe injury to Kuiper's right knee on June 1, 1980, required season-ending reconstructive surgery and undoubtedly shortened his career. "I didn't hurt when I came back, but I didn't have as much speed and I lost a lot of range," he said.

Kuiper, who was born and raised on his parents' dairy farm in Racine, Wisconsin, and his wife, Michelle, whom he married in 1985, have two children, son Cole, who was born in 1987, and daughter Dannon, born in 1989.

He was drafted by five teams (New York Yankees, the Seattle Pilots, Chicago White Sox, Cincinnati, and Boston) before the Indians, but he rejected all of them. It wasn't until after he went to Southern Illinois University, which he led to the College World Series finals (they lost to USC) in 1971, that he was picked by the Indians in the first round (21st overall) of the 1972 amateur draft (secondary phase) when he was 22.

"They gave me an $8,000 signing bonus, which was about half as much as the Yankees had offered earlier, but my dad and I figured I better take it because the word might get around that I didn't want to play pro baseball," he said.

Kuiper's peak salary after reaching the major leagues was $235,000 in each of his final six seasons, two with the Indians and four with the Giants which, as he said, "was pretty good at that time."

But Kuiper has no complaints, though he did when the Indians traded him to the Giants in November of 1981 for pitcher Ed Whitson. It did not turn out to be one of the Tribe's better deals.

"When I went to San Francisco, I left my heart in Cleveland," he once said.

When reminded of that comment, Kuiper said, "It wasn't that I didn't like San Francisco; I just didn't want to leave Cleveland. But how could I not be happy the way things have turned out for me and my family?"

No further clarification was necessary.

DICK
TIDROW

Pitcher, 1972–74

Best season: 1972, 39 games,
14-15 won-lost record, 0 saves,
2.77 ERA

Indians career: 85 games,
29-34 won-lost record, 0 saves,
3.78 ERA

It wasn't the worst trade the Indians ever made, but it certainly ranks among the bad ones, and also proves how financially unstable the franchise was in the bad old days, especially the 1960s and early 1970s. On April 27, 1974, general manager Phil Seghi sent Dick Tidrow, one of the Tribe's best young pitchers, and first baseman Chris Chambliss to the New York Yankees.

Tidrow was the Tribe's second winningest pitcher, second only to Gaylord Perry in each of the two previous seasons, in 1972 when Tidrow was a rookie, and again in 1973. Chambliss had been the American League's Rookie of the Year in 1971.

In exchange for Tidrow and Chambliss, and as seldom-used veteran reliever Cecil Upshaw, the Indians received four journeymen pitchers: starters Fritz Peterson and Steve Kline, and relievers Fred Beene and Tom Buskey.

It's interesting—and, perhaps, relevant—that the Yankees' general manager then was former Indians chief Gabe Paul, Seghi's longtime friend, boss, and mentor before leaving Cleveland a few months earlier to join George Steinbrenner in New York.

As it turned out, Tidrow and Chambliss went on to play prominent roles in the resurgence of the Yankees, who hadn't won a pennant since 1964, then captured three in a row from 1976 to 1978 and back-to-back World Series championships in 1977 and 1978.

As for the quartet of former Yankee pitchers, none distinguished himself in Cleveland, although Peterson, a 32-year-old southpaw whose best years were behind him, proved to be serviceable. He won 23 games while losing 25 during his two-plus seasons with the Tribe. He was sent to Texas in 1976 and retired later that season.

Kline, who'd been a promising young prospect before he developed arm trouble, went 3-8 in 1974 and never won another major-league game; Beene made 32 appearances in 1974 (with a 4-4 record, two saves), and 19 in 1975, his final season in baseball (1-0, one save); and Buskey, a workhorse in Cleveland—which is the best that could be said of his contributions—compiled a 12-13 won-lost record with a total of 25 saves in 161 games through 1977, and ended his career with Toronto from 1978 to 1980.

As much as anything, the deal in which Tidrow and Chambliss were lost to the Yankees proved that, not only were the Indians in severe financial trouble, their farm system was also bereft of pitching talent, and immediate help was needed.

The irrationality of the trade was punctuated in the fifth and deciding game of the 1976 A.L. championship series, when Chambliss hit a ninth-inning home run to beat the Kansas City Royals 7-6, and Tidrow was the winning pitcher in that pennant-winning game.

"I don't know if I'd call it the highlight of my career, but it certainly is one of my favorite memories," said Tidrow, who's still in baseball, though no longer in uniform. He is currently vice president of player personnel with the San Francisco Giants and works directly under General Manager Brian Sabean.

He scouted for the Yankees from 1985 to 1993, then joined the Giants as a scout in 1994, was promoted in 1996 to special assistant to the general manager (who then was former Indians farm chief Bob Quinn), became director of player personnel in 1997, and has been in his present position since 1998.

And even before he could be asked during the interview for this story—probably because the question arose so often at that time—Tidrow made it clear he would not have any comment concerning speculation that Barry Bonds is using or has been involved in the use of performance-enhancing drugs.

"For the record," he said, "there is nothing I can say. . . It is not something I should be commenting about . . . I actually had to sign a form [an affidavit] that says I will not talk about, you know, steroids in general."

When assured the questioning would not be steroid-oriented, Tidrow offered what amounted to a testimonial on behalf of the Giants slugger.

"[Bonds] may be is as good a hitter as I have ever seen," he said. "There's no doubt he is the best player, offensively, in the game today. He's got absolutely outstanding [vision]. His ability to hit balls in different parts of the strike zone is off the charts. And smart. He figures out how a pitcher is going to pitch to him and goes from there. At times you might think he has slowed up, but just when you do, all of a sudden he plays better. It seems anytime anybody knocks a part of his game, he concentrates on it and changes. That's how Barry is. If you start banging on one part of his game, pretty soon that part of his game looks pretty darn good."

Tidrow and his wife, Mari Jo, whom he married in 1976, have three children: daughter Rachelle, who was born in 1984, and sons Andy, born in 1980, and Matthew, in 1995. They live in Lees Summit, Missouri, and Tidrow commutes to San Francisco.

Born and raised in Hayward, California, Tidrow was a baseball, football, and basketball star in high school, attended Chabot Junior College in Hayward, and was selected by the Indians in the third round of the amateur draft (secondary phase) in 1967.

He climbed through the minor leagues to make it with the Indians in 1972, and was named the A.L. Rookie Pitcher of the Year by the *Sporting News.*

In 1972 and 1973, Tidrow's won-lost records were 14-15 and 14-16, and he pitched a total of 512 innings for the Indians, who won

"I was sad to leave the only organization I'd been with, but then I realized, when you get traded it's because somebody wants you."

only 72 and 71 games and finished in fifth and sixth place those seasons. Then, three weeks into the 1974 season, he was traded.

"I'm not sure what triggered it, though I know the Indians needed pitching depth at that time," said Tidrow. "I was sad to leave the only organization I'd been with, but then I realized, when you get traded it's because somebody wants you."

The following season, 1975, after Tidrow went a combined 12-12 as a starter with the Indians and New York, Bill Virdon, manager of the Yankees, put him in the bullpen. It proved to be an excellent move for Tidrow as well as the Yankees and, eventually, the Chicago Cubs.

Tidrow pitched in relief, usually as a set-up man for closer Sparky Lyle, although injuries to Catfish Hunter and Don Gullett forced the Yankees to return him to the rotation in 1978. After posting a 7-11 record in 25 starts, he went back to the bullpen.

The Yankees traded Tidrow to the Cubs on May 23, 1979, and in 1980 he led National League pitchers with 84 appearances. In 1983 he was traded to the Chicago White Sox and won two games that season, giving him a career total of 100 victories and 94 losses. Then, as a free agent in 1984, he signed with the New York Mets but lasted only a month, pitching in 11 games without a decision.

Still, it gave Tidrow the distinction of having been one of only two players in baseball history—Charlie Smith (1960–69) was the other one—to have played for both New York teams, the Yankees and Mets, and both Chicago teams, the White Sox and Cubs.

He appeared in 13 postseason playoff games, three in each of the World Series and ALCS with the Yankees (1976–78), and one in the 1983 ALCS with the White Sox. He was credited with one victory in the 1976 ALCS.

All of which, of course, wouldn't have happened for Tidrow if the financially strapped Indians hadn't been so desperate back then in 1974. It also begs the question: How much better might the Indians have been in subsequent years if, in 1974, they hadn't felt compelled to—as it turned out, *literally*—give away two of their best young players, both of whom became stars with other teams?

RAY
NARLESKI

Pitcher, 1954–58

Best season: 1955, 60 games, 9-11 won-lost record, 19 saves, 3.71 ERA

Indians career: 224 games, 39-21 won-lost record, 53 saves, 3.22 ERA

When he was young, during his six years in the minor leagues and even after making it big with the Indians in 1954, Ray Narleski was accused of "having an attitude," which in sports parlance means having a *bad* attitude.

And, guess what? As Narleski will tell you now, he still does.

"Back then," said Narleski, who with Don Mossi deserves credit for being the first of baseball's relief specialists, "what they called an 'attitude problem' was because I didn't appreciate the way I was being used, and I let them know I didn't."

"They," in this case, were Indians officials, headed by front-office chief Hank Greenberg and later Frank Lane. Included were manager Al Lopez and several others then in charge of the organization's minor-league teams going back to 1948, when Narleski signed with the Indians at the age of 19.

More specifically, Narleski didn't appreciate being employed as a relief pitcher. "In those days, relief pitchers were guys who were too old or not good enough to start," he said—and, of course, were paid accordingly.

"I was a very competitive guy, still am, and I wanted to be a starter because I knew I was good enough."

But now, because of the way the game has changed, relief pitchers—especially closers who are as good as Narleski and Mossi were—are an integral part of every team. They also are paid accordingly, and have been since the advent of free agency. All of which are reasons for whatever "attitude" problems Narleski still retains.

"I look at, and read about guys [pitchers] being clocked at 95 [mph] making big bucks and I think back to my career, when I was coming up to the Indians [and made it with them in spring training 1954].

"I truly believe my fastball was close to 100 [mph] and at times was above 100. I could feel the ball jump off my fingertips."

It was Birdie Tebbetts, then Narleski's minor-league manager at Class AAA Indianapolis, who first recognized Narleski's latent ability as a reliever. "One night [in 1953]," he said, "I pitched and lost a 12-inning game. I made a lot of pitches, and the next day I still threw batting practice. Birdie realized I was strong enough to do it and put me in the bullpen. I wasn't happy about it, but I was going on 25 and knew I'd soon be running out of time to make it to the big leagues, so I kept my mouth shut and did what I was told.

"The next spring [1954] the Indians took me to spring training, and I made up my mind that if I didn't make it, it would be my last year in pro baseball."

He made it. So did Mossi. Both as relievers.

It was Tebbetts who suggested that Lopez take a look at the two of them in relief, which probably was a good idea because the Indians had what turned out to be one of the best starting pitching staffs in the history of baseball: Bob Lemon, Early Wynn, Mike Garcia, Bob Feller, and Art Houtteman. They combined to win 93 games with 36 losses and, of course, Narleski and Mossi had much to do with their success.

The two relievers, the right-handed Narleski and the left-handed Mossi, made the team in spring training and their careers as relievers began, whether they liked it or not. Obviously, Narleski—*especially* Narleski—didn't like it.

"I accepted it because I had to, but I didn't get paid for it, and that's the part I didn't appreciate," he said. "I always felt I was underpaid."

In those days there was no such thing as a "save" statistic, which was a big reason relievers were, as Narleski lamented, under-appreciated and underpaid. "It wasn't until I left the game [in 1960] that people started talking about saves," he said.

A save rule was recognized as an official statistic beginning in 1969. Originally, a save was awarded to any relief pitcher who finished off a victory and was not credited with the win.

In 1973 the requirements were significantly tightened so that saves were only awarded if a pitcher either entered a game with the potential tying run on base, or at the plate, or pitched at least three effective innings while preserving the lead.

And in 1975 the rule was set to where it stands today: In order to earn a save, a reliever must finish off a victory without giving up the lead after entering the game with the potential tying run on base, at the plate, or on deck. Saves may also be earned by pitching effectively for three innings to preserve the victory without getting credit for the win.

Except for three spot-starting assignments in his first three seasons with the Indians (1954–56), Narleski labored almost exclusively in relief, appearing in 134 games. The next two years, under Kerby Farrell in 1957 and Bobby Bragan and Joe Gordon in 1958, he also started 39 games and worked out of the bullpen 51 times.

He and Mossi were traded by Frank Lane—who else?—to Detroit in November 1958 in what turned out to be one of the Tribe's worst-ever deals. The Indians received washed-up second baseman Billy Martin and pitcher Al Cicotte, who won a total of three games (with one loss) in 1959, his only season in Cleveland.

"I know why Lane traded me," said Narleski. "He was pissed off because whenever a reporter asked if I wanted to be a starter, I said, 'Yes.' I tried to tell Lane that I was only answering the same old question the same old way, but that wasn't good enough for him.

"I always came in with the tying or winning runs on base, but now a closer doesn't go into a game unless his team has a lead to protect, and then he needs only to pitch the last inning."

───────────────────

"What the hell, starters were making $40,000 in those days; my highest salary with the Indians was $15,000 [in 1958]. The Tigers gave me a $6,000 raise, but I couldn't produce for them [in 1959] because I hurt my back and couldn't get it fixed. Things were a lot different in those days."

After going 4-12 with the Tigers in 10 starts and 32 relief appearances in 1959, Narleski underwent back surgery for a ruptured disk. "My surgeon told me if I had waited another two weeks I would have lost the use of my legs."

The following spring the Tigers wanted Narleski to sign an affidavit absolving them of liability, but he refused. "When April 1 [1960] came and I wasn't covered by major-league baseball's medical plan, I walked out of spring training and went home."

And so ended Narleski's professional baseball career, though he continued to pitch on the sandlots in and around Philadelphia. "I got ten or twenty bucks a game," as a starter, of course, for the next three summers while working as a carpenter's helper.

His back problem was Narleski's second major injury. In the 1958 All-Star Game, he tore a muscle in his forearm during his 3⅓ inning stint against the National League.

"I came over the top with a curveball, and I could feel the pop, the muscle tearing," he said. "The rest of the season I couldn't straighten my arm until I soaked it in the whirlpool," though he continued to pitch, appearing in 44 games, compiling a 13-10 won-lost record.

Narleski pitched in an American League high 60 games in 1955, all but one in relief, with a won-lost record of 9-1. He also led the league with what would have been 19 saves (which were computed several years later, based on a rule implemented by baseball in 1969).

Retired and living in Camden, N. J., Narleski and his wife, Ruth, raised three sons, Ray Jr., Steve, and Jeffrey. Steve pitched in the Indians' farm system for eight years in the late 1970s and early 1980s, climbing as high as Class AAA.

"What really makes me want to tear my hair out is the kind of money that closers are making now, plus the fact that they don't face the same [problems] that I did. I always came in with the tying or winning runs on base, but now a closer doesn't go into a game unless his team has a lead to protect, and then he needs only to pitch the last inning."

You could almost hear Narleski shrug his shoulders in frustration when he said, "Mossi and I came along forty years too soon. I read a book recently about 'leveling the playing field' in baseball and, talking about salaries, the author had me [being worth] $8 million by today's standards. He also wrote that I would have won the Cy Young Award in 1955," which was the year *before* the award was given.

"But, what the hell, I had a great career. OK, I am bitter about a couple of things . . . and it's not just that they kept me in relief. If they had just paid me what I was worth, I would not have been pissed off about not starting, although I know I could have been successful and made a lot more money.

"If that's having an attitude, so be it. I had one."

And he still does.

DON
MOSSI

Pitcher, 1954–58

Best season: 1954, 40 games,
6-1 won-lost record, 7 saves,
1.94 ERA

Indians career: 224 games,
34-27 won-lost record, 32 saves,
3.34 ERA

The name is the same. Baseball is still baseball. Nine innings, three outs per inning, four balls constitute a walk and three strikes a strikeout.

But to Don Mossi, "It's a different game, entirely different, and if you want my opinion of modern day baseball, it sucks. It's not baseball the way we played it, and I liked it better back then, with one exception: the money players are paid today."

Mossi was the left-handed half of the outstanding two-man relief tandem with right-hander Ray Narleski that helped establish the Indians' pitching staff in 1954 as, arguably, the best ever.

The starters that season—Bob Lemon, Early Wynn, Mike Garcia, Bob Feller, and Art Houtteman received much of the credit for the Indians winning the pennant with 111 victories, then an American League record. But it might not have happened if not for Mossi and Narleski, who in 1954 appeared in more than half of the Tribe's games (Mossi 40, Narleski 42).

"The way Al used us," Mossi said, referring to manager Al Lopez, "depended on who was coming to the plate. If it was a left-hander, he brought me in. If it was a right-hander, he got Narleski." It gave

Lopez great flexibility because he could use either or both of them, depending on the situation.

Something else that was different in those days was that Lopez summoned either Mossi or Narleski as early as the seventh inning because both were capable of pitching several innings; closers today are expected to pitch only one inning, the ninth, to earn a save.

Back then, too—unfortunately for Mossi and Narleski—there was no official "save" rule in baseball; otherwise both undoubtedly would be better recognized for their contributions to the success of the Indians in 1954.

It wasn't until 1969 that a "save" rule became an official statistic. Four years later the rule was changed to make a save significantly easier to attain, and in 1975 the rule was set to where it stands today—in order to earn a save, a reliever must finish off a victory; he also can earn a save by finishing a victory without giving up the lead after entering the game with the potential tying run on base, at the plate, or on deck. A save also can be earned by pitching effectively for three innings to preserve the victory (without getting credit for the win).

All of which also is factored into Mossi's comparison of today's game with the way it was during his 12 years in the major leagues. He pitched for the Tribe from 1954 to 1958, the Tigers from 1959 to 1963, the Chicago White Sox in 1964, and the Kansas City Athletics in 1965.

"Actually, I think that players' records should be cut off somewhere along the line, separating baseball from the way it is, to the way it was," said Mossi. "Almost everything in the game is different now. The players are much bigger and so much stronger. Look at their necks, their arms. Is it because of steroids? I don't know. When we finished a season, we went home and got a job. But these guys [today] go to a health club and work out, or whatever they do to bulk up.

"I was watching a game on television the other day, and a batter got fooled on an inside pitch that almost hit him on the fists. He gave it one of those inside-out swings, damn near broke his bat on the ball, and hit it out of the park, even to the opposite field.

"Actually, I pay very little attention to baseball now. It's not interesting anymore. At times it even disgusts me. For me, it's no fun to watch.

"And the money guys are making. I guess it's the American way to get all you can. If it were me, money wouldn't be the only factor, not even the major factor. I'd be going for the conditions, where I would feel the best, the happiest. Hell, I'd cut the dollars in half just to be happy.

"It makes me wonder if baseball is pricing itself out of business. Where is it going to end? They just can't keep going the way it is going."

Mossi's peak salary was $27,500 with Detroit in 1962, after a 15-7 season as a starter in 1961. "Now guys are making that much every time at-bat," he said with disdain.

When Mossi signed with the Indians in 1949 as a 20-year-old amateur free agent in Daly City, California, he got a $2,000 bonus, "which I thought was great."

He was mildly successful as a starter in his five minor-league seasons and was placed on the Indians' major-league roster in 1954, primarily because of a rule then in effect: if Mossi hadn't been promoted, the Tribe would have been required to release him.

"That's when I met Ray [Narleski]," said Mossi. "I didn't have any high hopes of making it with the Indians that season, and I'm not sure if Ray did, either. We were just going through the motions and did the best we could in every chance we got to pitch."

And, virtually every chance they got, they pitched well. Lopez was impressed.

"It was kind of a freak thing that happened to me," said Mossi. "I had been a typical left-hander. I threw pretty hard, but I was wild. Then [coach] Mel Harder changed my grip on the ball and a couple other things, and all of a sudden my control was great.

"I think that players' records should be cut off somewhere along the line, separating baseball from the way it is, to the way it was."

"A few days before we were to break camp, I talked to Harder and told him, 'If I'm not going to Cleveland, I'm going home and get a job.' He said, 'Hang on. Just stick around,' and a couple days later the Indians told me and Narleski that we made the team.

"I'd always been a starter, but I didn't care if they wanted me to relieve, as long as I was in the big leagues, though I knew it bothered Ray. He always wanted to start. But it was good for the Indians to use us in relief, the way Lopez did, and it was good for us.

"I agree with those who say that Ray and I began the business of specialization, and the way relief pitchers are used now, either Ray or I could be what they call a 'set-up' guy and a 'closer.'"

Mossi's relationship with Narleski always was good. "We were roommates and the best of friends all the time we were together. We don't see much of each other anymore, but we exchange Christmas cards and still talk every once in a while."

Mossi lives in Caldwell, Idaho, with son Don Jr. He also raised two daughters, Deborah and Linda. His wife of 46 years, Eunice, died in 1995.

When Frank Lane traded the two pitchers, and utility infielder Ozzie Alvarez, for a washed-up Billy Martin and under-achieving pitcher Al Cicotte, Mossi said he initially was disappointed. "Your first thought is, 'Gee, why don't they want me anymore?' Then you realize you were wanted by the team that traded to get you, which makes it OK."

When Kerby Farrell replaced Lopez as the Indians' manager in 1957, he made Mossi a starter, after which he went 11-10. But he went back to the bullpen under Bobby Bragan in 1958. With the Tigers, from 1959 to 1963, he started again, then spent the last two seasons as a reliever with the White Sox and the Athletics. He finished his 12-year major-league career with a 101-80 won-lost record and a 3.43 ERA in 460 games, 295 as a reliever.

Among the 165 games he started were seven consecutive victories over the New York Yankees, including five straight in 1959 and two early in 1960, earning Mossi the nickname "Yankee Killer."

Mossi's former teammate Al Rosen speculated that it might have been his wide-sweeping curveball. "It never stops breaking," Rosen once said.

And the reason Mossi had such a good curveball—though he also said he didn't know why—might have been due to his crooked left arm, which previously caused him to fail an army physical.

He said that in the winter of 1953–54, "I went all through my physical for the draft and everything was OK—until the doctor asked me if anything bothered me. I told him my elbow did once in awhile, that sometimes it locked. They took some x-rays and I was rejected.

"The first time I noticed that I couldn't straighten my arm was in high school. It bothered me some, but not enough to stop me from pitching."

FRED
BEENE

Pitcher, 1974–75

Best season: 1974, 32 games,
4-4 won-lost record, 2 saves,
4.93 ERA

Indians career: 51 games, 5-4 won-lost record, 3 saves, 5.72 ERA

It was, as Fred Beene could best recall, "sometime around 2002 or 2003" that he and his brother took their mother to a movie on her 89th birthday. This was in Oakhurst, Texas, Beene's hometown, which is about 60 miles north of Houston.

"She didn't have anything that she especially wanted to see until she noticed that a baseball movie was showing. [She] wanted to go to it, probably because she thought my brother and I would like it, so that's where we went," related Beene.

The movie was *The Rookie*, starring Dennis Quaid, based on the true story of a left-handed pitcher named Jimmy Morris who'd been a 35-year-old high school science teacher and baseball coach when he was signed by the Tampa Bay Devil Rays in 1999.

Morris pitched at Class AAA Durham (North Carolina) that season and was impressive enough to earn a September call-up, as well as a place on the Devil Rays' major-league roster in 2000.

Beene, who pitched seven seasons in the major leagues, two of them with the Indians (1974 and 1975), said he initially had no idea what the movie was all about. "I don't think I even thought about it being about baseball," he said.

But when the movie started, Beene suddenly perked up and realized that he'd met Morris some twenty years earlier, and that they got to know each other quite well. So well, in fact, that when the credits ran at the end of the movie, Beene's name was on the list.

"Actually, it took me about 15 minutes to remember Morris, then it hit me," said Beene from his home in Oakhurst, where he and his wife, Carolyn, whom he married in 1965, raised two children, Darrell and Monica.

It was Beene who "discovered" Morris and convinced the Milwaukee Brewers to select him in the January 1983 amateur draft. They picked Morris in the first round, fourth overall, and gave him a $35,000 signing bonus.

"Jimmy was the first player I scouted after I retired, and [he] was hired by the Brewers," said Beene. He covered Texas for the Brewers for 20 years, through 2001.

"I knew Morris had had some arm trouble and was released [by the Brewers]. I lost track of him and didn't know Tampa Bay signed him. And I sure didn't know that his story was made into a movie until I saw the movie."

Morris pitched four years in the minor leagues before a shoulder injury robbed him of his 98 mph fastball. He was released in June 1987, then signed by the Chicago White Sox in 1988, but Morris quit again a year later when the arm problem recurred. He went back to college, got his teaching certificate, and coached the Reagan County (Texas) High School team.

It was while Morris was throwing batting practice to his high school players that his sore arm disappeared, his fastball returned, and—on a "dare," according to the movie—Morris went to a Tampa Bay tryout camp. Despite his age, he showed the Devil Rays enough to be offered a contract. And three months later, on September 18, 1999, Morris made his major-league debut, pitching in relief against Texas.

Of such things are movies made.

Morris appeared in 16 games for the Devil Rays in 2000 before he retired again at the end of the season without a won-lost record.

"My mother and brother were surprised—but no more than I was—when I told them the story," said Beene.

Beene's professional baseball career began in 1964 when he was 21. He was signed by Baltimore, spent five seasons in the minors, and pitched for the Orioles from 1968 to 1970.

At five feet nine inches tall and 160 pounds, Beene admitted that he'd "heard all the insults all my life, that I was too little, too short, that kind of stuff," which probably was a factor in his being designated a relief pitcher early in his career.

As it turned out, it was a role in which he excelled both with the Orioles and later with the Yankees, to whom he was traded in1972. With New York in 1973, Beene was 6-0 in 91 innings in 19 games with a 1.68 earned run average. "I averaged over six innings an appearance, and I loved pitching for [manager] Ralph Houk," he said. Soon thereafter, however, Beene's flourishing career hit a roadblock.

On April 26, 1974, he was traded to the Indians in a deal that was highly controversial among players and fans of both teams. Those who followed the Tribe of that era will recall that, too often, favorite players were sent elsewhere for financial reasons, though the deals usually were described by management as part of a "rebuilding" program.

Beene came to Cleveland with veteran starting pitchers Fritz Peterson and Steve Kline, and another reliever, Tom Buskey—and, of course, a bundle of cash, estimated between $100,000 to $200,000.

The Yankees received popular first baseman Chris Chambliss, rising-star pitcher Dick Tidrow, and fading reliever Cecil Upshaw.

And just as fans in Cleveland were upset that two of their favorite young players were traded before they could blossom for the Indians, fans of the Yankees—as well as the Yankee players themselves—also were unhappy despite the acquisition of Chambliss and Tidrow.

In a story that was never previously made public, Beene said, "I'll never forget how angry everybody was in our [New York] clubhouse when the deal was announced. It was sheer pandemonium. Everybody was in an uproar because they thought, by trading four pitchers, two of them [Peterson and Kline] regular starters, the Yankees were giving up on the season before it hardly got started.

"When Gabe Paul [then the Yankees' president] came into the clubhouse that night, everybody started shouting insults at him for breaking up the team. Two of the angriest guys were [team leaders] Thurman Munson and Elston Howard."

Beene, of course, also was upset. "I was crushed," he said. "I'd had a great season in 1973. I averaged over six innings an appearance and was used in super-long relief and felt I had finally established myself, that I'd earned a spot with what I'd done. And then I had to go somewhere else and establish myself all over again.

"Bill Virdon [the Yankees' manager] told me I had to be in the deal, that if I wasn't, Phil Seghi wouldn't make the trade."

It turned out great for the Yankees, but not the Indians—nor for Beene. "The Indians didn't use me right. I got out of my role and I let it bother me. I realized later that I behaved like a dummy after I got to Cleveland," he said. "You can say I pouted; I didn't act like a professional."

Beene went 4-4 in 32 relief appearances in 1974, then suffered an arm injury in mid-1975 that, essentially, ended his major-league career, though he went on to pitch in the minors through 1979.

He was the pitching coach for Class AAA Tidewater, a New York Mets farm club in 1980, then joined the Brewers as a scout and found Jimmy Morris—and twenty years later, when he went to the movies one night, Beene "found" Jimmy Morris again.

GARY
BELL

———

Pitcher, 1958–67

Best season: 1959, 44 games,
16-11 won-lost record, 5 saves,
4.04 ERA

Indians career: 419 games,
96-92 won-lost record, 45 saves,
3.71 ERA

Gary Bell was good, but never seemed to be as good as everyone thought he would be—or should be—throughout his nine seasons with the Tribe, and the two seasons after he left Cleveland.

Bell signed as an amateur free agent in 1955 at the age of 19 for a $4,000 bonus, made it to the Indians in 1958, and went 12-10 as a rookie. He was traded to Boston on June 4, 1967, was claimed by the Seattle Pilots in the expansion draft on October 15, 1968, and on June 8, 1969 was dealt to the Chicago White Sox, who released him four months later.

"If only he'd be a little meaner . . . if only he wouldn't be so easygoing, so laid back all the time." Those are things people in the Indians hierarchy often said when Bell's name was mentioned.

Perhaps the implied criticism was valid. Who knows? The only thing certain was that it didn't please Bell. Still doesn't.

"That's a lot of [bleep]. I heard too much of it. I got tired of it," he said with a scowl, and then reverted to his usual easy-going demeanor, which might have been a reason his nickname—"Ding-Dong"—was coined. Again, who knows?

"OK, so I horsed around. Still do. I laugh easily and I have fun. I don't take myself or anyone too seriously. But when I pitched, that was something else. I tried as hard as I could, and I wanted to win as badly as anyone.

"Would I have been a better pitcher if I'd destroyed some furniture in the clubhouse or kicked the dirt when somebody got a hit?"

Then, not waiting for an answer, he said, "That's baloney," or, actually, something more expressive.

"Nobody can change a person's personality. Nobody can teach somebody to be different. It would have been like your boss telling you to write like somebody else," he said to the scribe interviewing him. "That wouldn't have helped you." And then Bell paused again, the twinkle in his eyes returning, and said, "Well, maybe it would have helped you."

More vintage Bell.

His record with the Tribe was 96-92 with a 3.69 earned run average as both a starter and reliever. He started almost exclusively from 1958 to 1961, when he went 49-47, but from 1962 to 1965 Bell pitched out of the bullpen 216 times and started only 15 games.

Overall, including his stints with the Red Sox, Pilots, and White Sox, Bell won 121 games and lost 117. He had 71 complete games and 51 saves in 519 appearances, and a commendable 3.68 ERA.

"I hated relieving, but in those days you had no choice. You did what the manager told you to do," said Bell, who pitched for seven different managers during his nine-plus years with the Indians—Bobby Bragan, Joe Gordon, Jimmie Dykes, Mel McGaha, Birdie Tebbetts, George Strickland, and Joe Adcock. "I loved Gordon, and Dykes was a nice man, too. They were all OK, except for Adcock," said Bell.

It was on the subject of his overall record that Bell admitted having one regret.

"With the stuff I had, I think I was good enough to win at least 200 games," he said. "I'm not sure why I didn't, though I'm damned sure it wasn't because I wasn't mean enough."

"I don't know how hard I threw because they didn't have radar guns then, but I tell people they used a sun dial to time me," he quipped.

Then, serious again, he said, "I guess I got it up there in the mid- to high-90s [miles per hour]," which was a major reason for the high expectations the Indian chiefs had for Bell.

In Cleveland in 1967, before he was traded to the Red Sox, Bell was paid $27,000. "When I got to Boston, Dick O'Connell [the Red Sox general manager] asked me how much I wanted [to earn for 1968]," said Bell. "I could hardly get the words out of my mouth. Finally I said, kind of hopefully and very softly, '$40,000.' He told me, 'I'll give it to you if you promise you'll win 20 games.' I said, 'OK, I will,' and it was done."

So how many games did Bell win in 1968? "I was 11-11, but we won the pennant, and I got the same money the next year."

In the World Series in 1967, Bell pitched in three games against St. Louis, two in relief and one as the starter (and loser) in Game 3. He also earned a save in Game 6 before the Cardinals won Game 7.

When Bell retired from baseball after the 1970 season, he returned to his hometown of San Antonio, Texas, and "bounced around" in various jobs. In 1987 he started his own sporting goods business— Gary Bell Athletic Supplies—which he and his wife, Rhonda, operate. They were married in 1978 and have two children, daughter Casey and son Cody, both of whom attend Texas A&M University. Bell also has three children from a previous marriage.

"Things are going well," he said. "I had a heart attack in 1992, but I'm OK. It hit me when I woke up and felt sick one morning. It was like having a hangover, but I knew it was something more than that because I hadn't been drinking the night before.

"That's one advantage about being a drinker. You know when you're supposed to have a hangover—and when you're not. Anybody who doesn't drink wouldn't know."

He also plays a lot of golf. "I can still break 80 once in awhile," and said his handicap "depends on who I'm playing against."

Bell never aspired to get back into baseball as a scout, coach, or manager. "Back then scouts and coaches didn't make any money. And now, the game has gone by us so much, I'd be lost. When I pitched, you picked up the ball and threw it. Now it's all so technical. Everything is computerized . . . and complicated.

"And everybody is making so much money. It's hard to believe the contracts that guys are getting. It proves that the money always was there, but in my day the players didn't get much of it. Especially not if you played for guys like Frank Lane and Gabe Paul, which I did. They were really tight with a buck.

"After my first year with the Indians [1958], when I won 12 games and was making only the minimum, which at that time was $7,000—that's $7,000 a year!—I tried to get a raise out of Lane. I was going to hold out for $12,000, and he flat-out refused. He told me, 'We're going to start the season without you if you don't sign,' which scared the [bleep] out of me, so I signed. That's how it was."

As for the game today and the money that players are making, Bell said, "We're all jealous, all the old guys. But I don't have a problem with it. If the owners are stupid enough to pay guys $25 million a year, why not take it?

"We weren't even allowed to have an agent. If you had one, they [the owners] wouldn't talk to you. We had a guy named Jim Baxes, an infielder who came over from the Dodgers during the [1959] season, and his wife wanted to negotiate for him. But Lane refused to let her, and when the season ended, [Baxes] was gone.

"And when people ask me how much I think I could be making if I were playing now, I tell them I'd probably get four or five million a year. But then, I guess I'd have to scowl a lot, not smile as much as I did, and break up some furniture in the clubhouse to prove that I could be a mean guy, a nasty S.O.B. like everyone back there thought I should have been."

FRANK DUFFY

Shortstop, Third Base, Second Base, 1972–77

Best season: 1973, 116 games, .263 batting average, 8 home runs, 50 RBI

Indians career: 805 games, .233 avg., 26 home runs, 233 RBI

Frank Duffy helped clarify, albeit inadvertently, one of the enduring mysteries about Gaylord Perry.

The two players came to Cleveland in 1972 in what is regarded as one of the best trades the Indians ever made. The Indians dealt Sam McDowell to San Francisco for Perry and Duffy, after which Perry embellished his Hall of Fame credentials and Duffy became one of the best shortstops in the American League. McDowell's troubled career ended four years later, far short of all that had been expected of him.

Previously, Duffy had been unable to establish himself with either Cincinnati, where he played behind Dave Concepcion, or San Francisco, where he was slated to be an understudy to Chris Speier. But in Cleveland he took over at shortstop, replacing Jack Heidemann, who'd been injured and then traded. Duffy was soon appointed co-captain of the team and played well, especially in the field, through 1977.

Tribe fans know the great contributions Perry made to help keep the Tribe afloat in those financially unstable days of the franchise, before he was sent to Texas in 1975 in a deal designed to replenish the failing pitching staff.

They also know that, during his three and a half seasons with the Indians, Perry was regularly accused of throwing "spitballs" or "grease balls" or other aptly named illegal pitches.

But nothing was ever proven, and nobody ever shed any definitive light on the matter, except in Perry's book, *Me and the Spitter*, in which he teasingly "admitted" to sometimes throwing illegal pitches, though nobody was sure he was serious.

But recently Duffy was asked about playing behind Perry. The question came in a letter from an aspiring writer and longtime fan who contacted former Tribe players.

The man asked Duffy if he "could ever tell whether the pitch was a 'wet one' after the ball was hit to you." He also asked, "Did you ever have any difficulty handling one of those grounders?"

Duffy's written reply: "Oh yeah! The first time I got a ground ball off [Perry's] 'sinker' it slipped off my fingers for a throwing error. After that I always used three fingers to throw to first base if the ball was hit to me off a wet one [from Perry]. Not as much velocity, but much more accurate."

This is not to suggest that Duffy did not have great respect for Gaylord.

"I liked him mainly because we always had a heck of a good chance of winning when he pitched," Duffy said. "[Gaylord] was a great competitor, one of the fiercest competitors I ever played with or against, although his competitiveness sometimes was a negative. He always wanted to win so badly that, at times, he brutalized some of the guys on the team.

"Some of them sometimes deserved it. Everybody knows we had some guys who were not always alert and on top of their game."

Duffy, who was selected by Cincinnati in the first round of the amateur draft (secondary phase) in 1967 when he was 21, received a signing bonus of $30,000 after he graduated as a psychology major from Stanford University. He was a second team All-American shortstop and previously had been drafted by Atlanta in 1966.

Duffy's best season with the Indians was 1973, when he batted

"Overall, in Cleveland, we were just like a happy family, which is what I missed in Boston. Everything with the Red Sox was stratified."

.263 and won the Gordon Cobbledick Golden Tomahawk award as the team's most underrated player by vote of his teammates. In 1973 and 1976 he led American League shortstops in fielding.

Duffy and his second wife, Pam, whom he married in 1986, have two sons: Ryan, born in 1989, and Logan, born in 1992. He retired after being released by Boston in May 1979, a year and a half after he was traded by the Indians, and lives in Tucson, Arizona, where he owns his own real estate company, Duffy Realty.

Duffy said he "loved" playing Cleveland and "hated" Boston, though it was with the Red Sox that he made the most money, $88,000 in each of his last two years.

"Playing for the Indians was the epitome of my major-league experience," he said. "The [front office] wasn't real good . . . Nick Mileti and Ted Bonda had something like 97 or 98 partners [actually about 52], but playing with Buddy Bell, Jack Brohamer, Dennis Eckersley, and Duane Kuiper was like a family thing. Everybody pretty much felt equal."

What about George Hendrick? "Well, he didn't like talking to [the media], but he didn't bother us [players]. He could be sullen, I know, and there were times he didn't hustle and Gaylord got on him a lot. They didn't like each other, but you have to admit, Hendrick had a lot of talent.

"Overall, in Cleveland, we were just like a happy family, which is what I missed in Boston. Everything with the Red Sox was stratified. They had their superstars like Carl Yastrzemski, Fred Lynn, Jim Rice, and Carlton Fisk, then the rest of the starters, and then us [non-regulars]. We were like a bunch of utility guys and were treated like crap."

As for baseball today, Duffy said, "The steroids issue has really screwed up the records and will continue to do so until something is done, which is really unfortunate. It's certainly not a level playing field the way things are now.

"A big part of the problem is that, when most of your competition is doing it, you are almost forced to join them and do [steroids] too.

"I don't know the Players Association's stance on the issue, but they're probably against the strict enforcement of a testing program, and that's a shame—though I hate to go against the association because they have done so much good for the players.

"When I played I was always supportive [of the Players Association], but I think it's time that something needs to be done."

When Duffy was asked about the speculation that Barry Bonds is and has been a user of steroids, he avoided a direct implication of the San Francisco slugger.

"All I can tell you," he said, "is that I think Bonds is the greatest player I have ever seen. He obviously is a great hitter for average and power, and a great clutch hitter, although he no longer is a great outfielder or great base stealer as he once was.

"I can't believe what a great [batting] eye he has, and how disciplined he is. I have never seen a hitter, especially a power hitter, who is so disciplined, who will take a walk after walk instead of just swinging at balls out of the strike zone. Every other power hitter I've seen gets frustrated and gives himself up. But not Bonds. I've never seen him do that. It's just incredible. And that's just him."

As for the continuing escalation of salaries in major-league baseball, Duffy said: "It doesn't bother me because it's all relative. By that I mean [that] when I played, guys like me made more money than Rocky Colavito, and that wasn't fair. It's just the way it was.

"By the same token, I can't complain that players today are making so much more than when I played. If that's what the market will bear, it's what the owners will pay.

"If it gets to be too big and the fans start cutting back [in buying tickets], I suppose baseball will have to make some adjustments. But the teams are still drawing well and they continue to get big TV contracts, so I don't see any major problems yet.

"What I do hate to see is how baseball is losing parity—when a team like the Yankees, year after year, can sign all the free-agent superstars they want. That I don't like. I don't know why the commissioner allows something like that.

"I think it is ridiculous [that] we really don't have an impartial commissioner; we've got an owner who is the commissioner. What we need is a guy who would dare to do what's best for both sides, players and owners, not one who works for the owners and is himself an owner, or allegedly a *former* owner. It's a joke to say he is the commissioner."

DUKE
SIMS

———

Catcher, First Baseman, Outfielder, 1964–70

Best season: 1970, 110 games, .264 batting average, 23 home runs, 56 RBI

Indians career: 536 games, .236 avg., 76 home runs, 216 RBI

It is safe to assume that few major-league baseball players enjoyed life more than Duke Sims. He has said of his career: "It was a blast, from the first day to the last."

It also is safe to assume that few major-league baseball players ever worried less about his own image, of how he was perceived by the media or the fans. "What you saw is what you got," he has said.

As Sims once told manager Birdie Tebbetts early in his career with the Indians, "There is nothing invisible about me."

And the best one-word description of Sims might be—*probably* is—irrepressible, even at times irreverent, which is OK with him.

That's not to say that Sims did not take the game seriously, was not a good player, or that he didn't always try hard as a catcher/first baseman for the Indians, and later the Los Angeles Dodgers, Detroit, the New York Yankees, and Texas.

He did. All of the above. It's true, as he also said, "I never took a short step between the lines."

Off the field, well, "Let me just say I had fun," said Sims.

It was then that Sims related some advice he received from Tebbetts, who was manager of the Indians from 1963 to 1966.

"Birdie called me into his office one day and said I had a reputation for running around," said Sims. "I told him, 'I'm a single guy.' He said, 'Well, you need to start going to bed and getting your rest.' I told him, 'When you start putting me in the lineup, I'll start going to bed and getting my rest.'"

Tebbetts started putting Sims in the lineup and, presumably, Sims started going to bed and getting his rest.

At least Sims's record indicates as much in his 10-plus seasons in the major leagues. He was signed by the Tribe as an amateur free agent in 1959, spent six seasons in the minors, and made it to Cleveland to stay in 1966 after brief trials in 1964 and 1965.

Sims's career batting average was .239 (though he insists it should have been higher) and he also was a better-than-average catcher with a good arm and decent power. Included in his statistics are 100 home runs and 310 RBI.

It was on the subject of his .239 batting average that Sims, despite his often-irreverent attitude, indicated the great pride he took in his accomplishments on the field.

"I got screwed out of a hit in a game against the Yankees in 1968," he said. "Steve Barber threw me a nasty, sidearm, low and inside fastball that I crushed. I hit a shot at [second baseman] Horace Clarke that handcuffed him and went through his legs.

"The inept scorer called it an error. An error! I couldn't believe it. Neither could Clarke. But it stood. And because it did, my [career] batting average wound up as .2394 [on 580-for-2,422]. And when it was rounded off, it was rounded off—*down*—to .239. If I had gotten credit for that hit, as I should have, my average would have been .2398, and rounded off—*up*—to .240." *(Note: The "inept" official scorer to whom Sims referred was Russell Schneider—yes, the author of this book—and it says here, the play was called correctly.)*

Regardless of Sims's complaint, it also says here—again—that he was a good player who always tried hard and, indeed, never took a short step on the field.

Sims and his wife, "Sonnie," (short for Sandra), were married in

1974 and have a daughter, Kirsten, born in 1976. They live on a golf course in Las Vegas.

Sims retired as a player in 1975 and 11 years later, in 1986, was offered a minor-league managing job by his former teammate, Ken (Hawk) Harrelson, then general manager of the Chicago White Sox.

"I wanted to get back in the game, but I probably was away from it too long and had lost track of what was happening," said Sims. He managed the White Sox farm clubs at Appleton, Wisconsin, and also Newport News, Virginia, though not for long.

"I liked being on the field, but I didn't like the kids. Too many of them are spoiled. I tried to instruct them, help them, but they thought they knew more than I did," he said. "I learned that base-ball is the only industry in the world [in which] wisdom is not ac-cepted by the people who don't know anything.

"I thought I did a good job, that I was a good manager. But I couldn't take the kids. Most of them, anyway." It was Sims's only season back in baseball.

Which broached the subject of the game today, including the wild escalation of salaries since his playing days and also specula-tion about the rampant use of steroids. "First, let me tell you that I made $55,000 in 1974, the year I played for the Rangers, but that was by far my biggest salary," he said. "I figured out once that Alex Rodriguez [whose average annual salary in 2006 was over $21 mil-lion] made more in one at-bat [approximately $36,000] than I did most of the years I played.

"One season with the Indians, when Joe Azcue and I both were on the team, I was getting about $16,000 and Joe was probably making $25,000. I told Joe that we should hold out together for a combined $100,000, that our position, catcher, was worth $100,000 because Johnny Bench had just signed with Cincinnati for one-hundred grand. The Indians needed either one of us and couldn't do without both of us. That way each of us would get $50,000, but if Gabe Paul negotiates with us individually, he'll break us apart and say that neither of us is worth $50,000.

"But [Azcue] wouldn't go along with it. 'Oh, roomie,' he said. 'I got two kids and they might release me. I cannot take that chance.' So I held out alone and got something like $18,000 or $19,000 from Gabe."

As for the salaries that players are receiving today, Sims said, "I think it's fabulous. I also think the owners are stupid. I mean, if you offer [millions of dollars] to me, am I going to say no to it? Hell, no, I'm not.

"What it amounts to is millionaires fighting with billionaires."

And the steroids issue? Sims never hesitated. He said, "If they [steroids] had been around in my day, I would have been into them up to my eyeballs—before major-league baseball put in rules against them—which apparently is what a lot of guys did.

"For one year, to get a $15-million contract or even a $5-million deal by beefing up—and if there were no rules against it, which there weren't—hell yes, I would take a shot at it. The way money was being thrown around, I don't blame guys for doing it. They are hired guns. They get paid to play and perform. And if you get paid as a professional to perform as a professional athlete, you are going to do everything you possibly can to enhance your career.

"I knew Lyle Alzado [of the Browns, 1979–81], that he was on [steroids] and died a terrible death at an early age. That's the risk guys are taking. When you are young and an athlete, you feel like you are bulletproof, that you have an 'S' on your chest like Superman.

"So, I'll say it again, yes, I probably would have done it [used steroids]. But I would have gotten the money they were paying me and got off the stuff."

And, in Sims's opinion, if it turns out—if it is proved—that Barry Bonds was on steroids, would his records be "tainted"?

"Everything is tainted," he said. "[Bonds] still has to hit the ball, and he also has to hit it against a lot of guys who probably are doing the same thing, taking the same stuff."

That's vintage Duke Sims. Irrepressible. Irreverent. And outspoken. Especially outspoken.

EDDIE
LEON

Second Baseman, Shortstop
1968–72

Best season: 1970, 152 games,
.248 batting average, 10 home runs,
56 RBI

Indians career: 442 games,
.243 avg., 21 home runs, 126 RBI

When he graduated with honors from the University of Arizona in 1966 at the age of 21, Eddie Leon had a difficult choice: accept an attractive offer with a Tucson, Arizona, engineering firm, or play minor-league baseball in the Indians' farm system.

"Actually, looking back at it, it was easy," said Leon, who's now the president of one of the most successful engineering firms in Tucson and, as such, has been deeply involved in real estate development in southern Arizona since 1985.

He chose to sign with the Indians, who'd selected him in the second round of the 1967 amateur draft (secondary phase), and embarked upon a baseball career that began in Portland, Oregon, in 1967.

"I had my degree," he said, "but a baseball career is what I wanted more than anything." He got it in Cleveland and later with the Chicago White Sox and New York Yankees in the major leagues, and finally in Mexico in 1976–77.

"I always loved baseball and always was pretty good at it," he said from his office at the Leon, Taylor Management firm in Tucson, where in addition to his engineering business he is active in many civic endeavors.

Leon was much more than "pretty good" at baseball at the University of Arizona, which he attended on academic and athletic scholarships. He won All-America honors three years (1964–66) as a shortstop for the Arizona Wildcats, whom he helped lead to the NCAA College World Series during his senior year. He also was a member of the United States team that played in the World Amateur Baseball Tournament in Hawaii in 1966.

Leon made his major-league debut on September 9, 1968, late in his second season in professional baseball; midway through 1969 he was promoted from Portland of the Class AAA Pacific Coast League to be the Indians' regular shortstop.

They switched him to second base in 1970, a move that disappointed Leon, but he adapted and went on to have his best season. He played for the Tribe through 1972, when he was traded to the White Sox. Two years later he was dealt to the Yankees, then ended his major-league career in 1975.

But not his baseball career.

Leon had offers to play Triple-A ball in both Hawaii and Japan but instead chose to go to Mexico, where he played two years (1976–77) for Tampico in the summer league, and for Hermosillo in the winter.

"Looking back at it, it probably was the wrong decision, because once you get to that league you basically are done. But at the time I thought it was a way to continue playing and maybe do well enough to get back to the big leagues," he said.

But that didn't happen. "I was pretty much a star [in Mexico] because I had once played for the Yankees. I got paid about $10,000 a month, which was good because back then the average salary in the big leagues was something like $35,000 [a season].

"I enjoyed it because it was still baseball, but you really have to love the game to play down there. We won two championships, but it was an eye-opening experience.

"I joined Tampico on a Sunday and, because I hadn't played in about two months, I told the owner and the manager I needed a little time to get in shape. That was OK, except that when I got to the park they gave me a uniform and said, 'Oh, just play a few innings . . . the fans want to see the guy we just signed who played for the Yankees.' So I did, except that it turned out to be 14 innings, a double header, not just a couple innings.

"When the game was over and I went in to take a shower—under the only one that worked—I asked for a towel and they told me everybody had to provide his own, just like we also had to provide our own sanitary socks and undershirts.

"They told me we didn't have another game for three days, and I thought I'd have a chance to go to the beach or somewhere to relax and rest my sore arms and legs—until the manager told me to hurry because the bus would be leaving soon.

"When I asked, 'Where are we going?' he told me we had a game Wednesday in Juarez, which was a 40-hour bus trip from Tampico. I offered to fly there, at my own expense, which I did, but I couldn't get into the hotel until the team arrived. So I stayed with a friend in El Paso [Texas], which is right across the Rio Grande from Juarez.

"And thank God I did. As it turned out, the team didn't arrive until Wednesday afternoon because the bus had broken down a couple of times en route.

"That's what it was like playing in Mexico," said Leon.

But, as he said, it was still baseball, so he played two years down there—and played pretty well—all the while hoping to get back to the big leagues, though the opportunity never came.

"Actually, once I got used to it, once I realized I had to have my own socks, undershirt, and towel—and do my own laundry—it wasn't all that bad. It was still baseball."

Leon returned to Tucson in 1978, took a job as a civil engineer, and in 1980 started his own company, which is thriving. His partner—the "Taylor" part of Leon, Taylor Management—is his wife, Joy, whose maiden name was Taylor. He is president, she is vice-president. They were married in 1985 and have a son, Alex, born in 1987. Leon also had two sons, Eddie Jr. and Danny, with his first wife, Marilyn.

*"Once I got used to [the Mexican League], once
I realized I had to have my own socks, undershirt, and towel—and do my own laundry—it
wasn't all that bad. It was still baseball."*

"I have been doing a lot of different things since I retired from baseball," said Leon. "Primarily, I'm building subdivisions for sale to either individual home owners or to builders who want to buy a plot of land and build one- or two-hundred houses."

"There are 19 or 20 developments around [Tucson] that I can drive by and say, hey, I designed and built the subdivisions and the infrastructure for those developments. I get great satisfaction in what I am doing. I am making money and I am happy." He added, "Hey, it's almost as good as playing baseball."

Leon also has played a key role in returning major-league baseball to Tucson for spring training after the Indians pulled out and moved to Florida in 1993. Since then the Arizona Diamondbacks, Chicago White Sox, and Colorado Rockies train in Tucson.

"We'd like to get the Indians to return, and they have shown some interest. They're shopping around and a lot obviously depends on what [deal] they're able to get in Florida, or somewhere else," he said.

On the subject of baseball, Leon said he had a couple of offers to coach or manage in the minors before he played in Mexico, "but at that time nobody except the owners were making any money in the game. Now it's different. I often wish I had come along thirty years later. I could sit on the bench as well as anyone for the kind of money they're paying now." His peak major-league salary was $35,000 with the Yankees in 1975.

"What is happening in baseball is scary," he said. "It can't keep going the way it is. Things have got to reverse somehow, someway, though I don't know if that's possible.

"When we went through the first strike [in 1972], what we [the Players Association] wanted were increases in our benefits, and at that time the union was willing to accept a salary cap. We were telling the owners, 'We'll take only this much of the proceeds [revenues] if you will improve the benefits to this and this and this. But the owners, because they'd had their way for close to one hundred years, didn't think they needed to do anything, and neither did they think they were going to lose in negotiations or in a strike. They just put their heads in the sand and didn't pay attention to what was happening, and that's what turned the tide to what is now the case.

"And what is now the case is that the pendulum has swung the other way, and it seems to me now it's the players who have their heads in the sand. They don't seem to realize what they've got and what they stand to lose.

"They're making the same mistake the owners did . . . except that now there are more zeroes behind the dollars.

"If you love the game as I do, it's scary," he said again.

KEN
SUAREZ

Catcher, 1968–69, 71

Best season: 1969, 36 games,
.294 batting average, 1 Home Run,
9 RBI

Indians career: 103 games,
.234 avg., 2 home runs, 18 RBI

Ken Suarez was a catcher for three major-league teams, including the Indians (1968–71), as well as the Kansas City Athletics and Texas Rangers before and after his service in Cleveland.

He appeared in only 103 games and batted 218 times in three seasons with the Tribe (he was idled with a broken leg in 1970). He spent most of his time catching pitchers in the bullpen while backing up Joe Azcue, Duke Sims, and Ray Fosse.

But that's not to say Suarez didn't contribute to the limited success the Indians experienced in those days when the fans' springtime optimism usually gave way to disappointment and frustration by midseason.

In a story that couldn't be told back then, Suarez, in addition to his position on the field, also saw duty in right field—actually in the right field *grandstand.* That's where Suarez, wearing street clothes, often sat with a pair of high-powered binoculars for what he called "selected" games.

On those occasions it was his job, as assigned by manager Alvin Dark, to pick off the opposing catcher's signs and relay the information—whether the next pitch would be a fastball or breaking ball—to the Tribesman at the plate.

"We didn't do it all the time, just for selected games, depending on the [opposing] pitcher," Suarez said from his home in the Dallas-Fort Worth area, where he works for a company that manufactures and distributes agricultural products.

Because he'd been selected by the Indians from Kansas City in the minor-league draft the previous winter, Suarez had to be kept on the major-league roster a full season in 1968 or be offered back to the Athletics at a reduced price. And to earn his keep—and, of course, retain his place on the Tribe's roster—Suarez said he usually had to do anything that nobody else on the team wanted to do.

"Azcue and Sims were doing the catching then [in 1968 and 1969], and I was the low man on the totem pole," said Suarez, who played 50 games behind Fosse in 1971.

Sometimes, depending on where they were playing, Suarez did his espionage from the Indians' bullpen.

Whether he was spying from the grandstands or the bullpen, "I had no problem seeing the [catcher's] signs, and no problem figuring out the pitch that was being called," said Suarez. "The problem was how to tell the batter, or signal somebody in our dugout who'd relay [the information] to the batter."

And before you ask the obvious question, Suarez answers it.

"It didn't bother me because a lot of teams were doing the same thing. When I played for Kansas City [in 1966 and 1967] we caught [White Sox manager] Eddie Stanky doing it in Chicago. His spy also was a catcher, a guy named Buddy Booker who 'worked' from the bullpen.

"Later, when I was with Texas [in 1972 and 1973], we discovered the Milwaukee Brewers were stealing, or *trying* to steal our signs. Does that make it OK? I don't know. You'll have to answer that question. I suppose a lot of fans . . . well, *some* fans . . . would consider it wrong," though Suarez didn't, nor did most of his peers.

Certainly, neither did the American League– and World Series–champion Indians of 1948, whose spy in the scoreboard at the old Municipal Stadium was either Bob Lemon or Bob Feller.

In the book *The Boys of the Summer of '48* Feller was quoted as saying, "All's fair in love and war—and in baseball, when you're trying to win a pennant."

Suarez said there was only one time that he almost got caught. "We were in Boston. I was in the bleachers at Fenway Park when a couple of cops came out there looking around. The Red Sox clubhouse guy must have alerted them to be on the lookout for me.

"When I saw the cops coming I picked up and ran out of the park, jumped in a cab, and told the driver to take me to the train station or some place where there were lockers that could be rented so I could stash the binoculars and get them later.

"The next day, a Saturday afternoon game, [Red Sox manager] Dick Williams had the phone from our dugout to the bullpen disconnected, probably because the cops didn't catch anybody in the bleachers. He thought we needed the phone to relay the information to our hitters."

But that didn't stop Suarez. Actually, it motivated him. "After I warmed up our starting pitcher [in the bullpen], I walked across the field to our dugout. I made sure everyone could see me carrying my glove with the case for the binoculars slung over my shoulder.

"But instead of the binoculars, I stuffed three or four baseballs in the case and, sure enough, almost on cue, Ron Luciano, one of the umpires, came running toward me.

"'What the hell do you think you're doing?' he yelled at me. 'You're going to get it from the commissioner,' and grabbed the binocular case.

"I said, as innocently as possible, 'What's wrong?' and handed him the case. He opened it and couldn't believe his eyes when he found the baseballs—but no binoculars. So much for the only time I ever came close to getting caught."

Otherwise, Suarez was the first to admit that his seven-year major-league career was very unspectacular. "When you're the smallest guy in the league, you do whatever needs to be done to stay in the game."

The most games Suarez played in any season were 93 for Texas in 1973, when he batted .248 and earned his highest salary, $20,000.

That also was the season Suarez spoiled a perfect game on June 16 for Baltimore's Jim Palmer, who retired the first 25 batters before Suarez singled with one out in the ninth inning.

Despite his stature, Suarez was known as a thinking man's catcher, which probably was another reason Dark chose him to be a spy for the Tribe.

Two of Suarez's high school and amateur baseball teammates in Tampa during the early 1960s were Lou Piniella and Tony LaRussa, both of whom became major-league players and championship-winning managers. Also, Suarez was related through marriage to the late Hall of Fame manager Al Lopez, whose niece, Irene, is Suarez's wife. They were married in 1965 and raised two daughters, Denise and Kendra.

Suarez played for Florida State University, was voted a first team All-American catcher in 1964, and was a member of the United States Olympic team—all despite his pint size.

It was Piniella, in his recent book, who lauded Suarez for being one of the smartest players he'd ever been around. But managing, or even coaching in the big leagues, was a job that Suarez never coveted. "I didn't want to pay the dues to get there," he said.

"For a long time [after he retired in 1974] I was bitter . . . not bitter at baseball, but bitter at all the B.S. you have to put up with when you're in the game. I loved the players and I loved baseball—still do—but it was all the crap that goes on behind the scenes.

"I'm often asked if I regret that I came along twenty or thirty years too early, before players were making the big money they're making now. My answer always was—and is—that I loved my career and my time in baseball. Anybody can get to the big leagues if they have the ability, but I did it without great ability.

"Oh, I was a good catcher, and I studied the game. But when you're five-foot-eight, you have to do a lot of things to get to the big leagues and stay there."

Which Suarez did, with a pair of binoculars—if not a big bat.

JIM
KERN

Pitcher, 1974–78, 1986

Best season: 1976, 50 games, 10-7 won-lost record, 15 saves, 2.37 ERA

Indians career: 201 games, 30-31 won-lost record, 46 saves, 3.44 ERA

His teammates called him "Emu" because, by Jim Kern's own admission, "I was big and ugly and made funny noises, like an emu.

"I am still big and ugly—actually *bigger*, now I'm six foot five and 230 instead of six foot five and 170—though I don't make funny noises anymore, and my red beard is now gray."

And before you look it up, an "emu," the dictionary says, "is a large, non-flying Australian bird, rather like an ostrich."

Presumably, now that Kern is eligible for membership in AARP as a respected businessman in Arlington, Texas, he's no longer the sometimes off-the-wall character he, as Emu, was in his heyday.

"The emu stuff began in 1976," Kern said, "when Fritz Peterson and Pat Dobson were with us. One Sunday morning in the clubhouse they were working on a crossword puzzle, and I was doing my usual crazy stuff, running around crowing and flapping my arms. One of the clues in the crossword puzzle was the name of the world's largest non-flying bird.

"It was an emu," said Kern, and from then on, because Peterson and Dobson thought he resembled the dictionary's definition of the big bird, Kern was known as "Emu."

Emu subsequently also became the strange but distinctive name of Kern's company, "Emu Outfitting," which he started in 1987. "I had been a hunter and fisherman all my life, so it was a natural extension for me," he said. "We run hunting and fishing trips to Alaska, Zambia, South Africa, Uruguay, Argentina . . . actually, almost any place you might want to go to hunt and fish."

Kern and his wife, Jan, whom he married in 1970, raised three children—Jason, born in 1973, Ryan in 1977, and Emily in 1984—and recently became grandparents.

Jan, a software engineer, works for a high school in Arlington as director of technology.

After he rejected a "sort of" offer as a minor-league pitching coach following his release by the Indians in 1986, Kern's only involvement in baseball was as an analyst on television for some college and Rangers games from 1987 to 1999.

Kern signed with the Tribe for a $1,000 bonus as an amateur free agent at the age of 18 in 1967, and reached the major leagues after six and a half years in the minors and one year (1969) on active duty with the Marine Corps Reserves.

Between the beginning of his career in Cleveland in 1974 and its end 13 years later in 1986, also with the Indians, Kern pitched for Texas (1979–81), Cincinnati (1982), Chicago White Sox (1982–83), Philadelphia (1984), and Milwaukee (1984–85).

Described by one source as "an eccentric, intelligent prankster . . . whose overpowering fastball and lunatic reputation made him an intimidating short reliever," Kern averaged 8.6 strikeouts per nine innings from 1976 to 1979 when he won 41 games and saved 75.

The Tribe traded him to Texas at the end of 1978 in a deal for pitcher Len Barker and outfielder Bobby Bonds, and in 1979 Kern put together the best won-lost record of his career. He went 13-5 with 29 saves and a 1.57 earned run average, and was the co-winner of the American League Fireman of the Year award with Mike Marshall.

It also was in 1979 that Kern teamed with Sparky Lyle in the Rangers' bullpen. They came to be called "Craziness, Inc.," for their antics on and off the field.

But it turned out that 1979, when he earned his peak major-league salary of $325,000, was his last good season. Kern struggled in 1980 and 1981, when he re-injured his elbow, which he first hurt in 1976. Texas traded him the following winter to the New York Mets, who in turn sent him to Cincinnati, where he was so unhappy that he forced a trade by growing a beard that broke the Reds' unwritten "no facial hair" rule.

In August of 1982 he was dealt to the White Sox, and a month later, pitching in his 13th game for Chicago, Kern blew out his elbow. As one writer described it, "His elbow actually exploded . . . you could hear it all the way up in the press box."

Kern said, "That's when my arm retired, though I didn't" because he flat-out refused to quit. He underwent surgery and was disabled for a year and a half. "They put four hundred or so stitches on the inside of my elbow. I was in a cast for six months and a brace for another four months," said Kern.

By then he knew the end was near but tried to ignore the obvious, and he got a tryout with the Phillies without letting them know his arm still hurt. They were impressed and, on June 3, 1984, signed him to a contract worth $150,000 through the end of the season.

"Every time I pitched, my elbow swelled up the size of a baseball," he said, "and I'd spend the night sitting in my hotel room drinking a six pack of beer with my arm soaking in a sink full of ice for two or three hours.

"Basically, the reason I hung on was because at that point I had eight years and 156 days of major-league time [in the pension plan]," he said. "And, since 172 days constituted a full season, I needed one year and 16 more days to reach the 10 years that would give me the maximum pension benefits. I got it, though it took me three more years and four more teams to do so."

Released by the Phillies six weeks after they signed him, Kern

"Rick Waits once told me I was 'royalty.' He nicknamed me 'The Count of One Behind' because I was always pitching behind in the count.

---

caught on with the Brewers for the final two months of 1984, was released that winter, but re-signed with them and pitched through mid-June of 1985, until he was released again.

But he still wouldn't quit. He rehabbed some more, and the Indians took him back in 1986, perhaps as a favor. He appeared in 16 games in relief, won a game and lost one before he was released once and for all on June 17. It gave Kern five days more than he needed to reach 10 years in the pension plan.

"I've never regretted not pursuing a coaching job because, to me, my baseball ability was something that was given to me by the good Lord, even though, the truth be told, I wasn't a good athlete and I probably wouldn't have been a good coach," said Kern.

"I was what I called a 'one-trick pony.' I could throw hard, but I wasn't a pitcher. Actually, I was a horse-[bleep] pitcher, but a helluva thrower, which was the reason for whatever success I had."

For whatever reason, Kern had considerable success, though it isn't completely reflected by his career statistics. Almost exclusively a reliever—only 14 of his 416 pitching appearances were as a starter—Kern's career won-lost mark was 53-57 with 88 saves and a 3.32 ERA.

All but two of Kern's 14 starts were for the Indians from 1974 to 1978, and the only complete game he ever pitched was the first one he started in the major leagues, on September 6, 1974, a 1-0 loss to Baltimore.

"I threw hard, in the upper 90s [mph] consistently, and had a real forgiving arm in that I could pitch night after night." Then injury problems plagued and finally caught up with Kern. "But I was good once upon a time," he said, which he certainly was.

"My biggest problem was that I was wild, but sometimes wildly effective, if you know what I mean. Not too many batters dug in on me. I tell everybody I was so wild in the minor leagues that I got credit for a no-hitter when I didn't hit anybody. And as Rick Waits once told me, I was 'royalty,' and he nicknamed me 'The Count of One Behind' because, he said, I was always pitching behind in the count.

"I did not have good control. My pitches were always coming in a hurry . . . the question always was, where were they going?"

Kern—or "Emu," if you will—had this parting comment: "I am rather proud of collecting four pink [release] slips at the major-league level because it means they figured me out once—but I tricked them three times."

Which he certainly did, and he's pleasantly reminded of it every month when his pension check arrives in the mail.

JEFF
MANTO

Third Baseman, First Baseman, Outfielder, Catcher, 1990–91, 1997–98, 1999, 2000

Best season: 1990, 30 games, .224 batting average, 2 home runs, 14 RBI

Indians career: 77 games, .216 avg., 4 home runs, 27 RBI

It seemed the Indians could never make up their mind about Jeff Manto. They acquired him one way or another six times and subsequently let him go six times, either via a trade, waiver deal, outright release, or free agency.

"I loved it in Cleveland . . . but then, I loved it everywhere I wore a baseball uniform, especially a major-league uniform," said Manto, who's now wearing one as the batting coach for Pittsburgh in the National League.

"I never had a bad day in the major leagues—though I never had many," he said.

Manto's career statistics, 1985–2000, read like a Greyhound Bus schedule. In his 16-year professional baseball career, Manto played for 24 teams and, at one time or another, belonged to 12 major-league organizations—California Angels, Atlanta, Philadelphia, New York Mets, Baltimore, Boston, Seattle, Toronto, Detroit, New York Yankees, Colorado, and the Indians. He also played for a team in Japan. His stops in Cleveland included 120 games from 1990 to 1991, 1997 to 1998, again later in 1998, on two separate occasions in 1999, and finally in 2000.

Selected by the Angels in the 14th round of the 1985 amateur draft at the age of 20, Manto went on to play 289 major league games in parts of nine seasons, accumulating more than four years in the MLB pension plan.

And though he was never a star or even an everyday player at the major-league level, Manto batted .275 with 243 home runs and 921 RBI in 1,356 minor-league games.

His Indians odyssey began on January 9, 1990, when the Angels traded him to Cleveland for pitcher Scott Bailes. He was released on November 27, 1991, then re-acquired by the Tribe in a June 6, 1997, deal with the Blue Jays. He was selected off waivers by the Tigers on April 24, 1998, signed with the Indians as a free agent on June 16, 1998, was released by the Tribe on October 15, 1998, then re-signed with the Indians as a free agent on January 5, 1999. After being selected off waivers by the Yankees on July 2, 1999, he re-signed again with the Tribe on April 30, 2000, and was granted free agency on October 18, 2000.

When John Hart was general manager of the Indians, he called Manto "our Crash Davis," a reference to the perennial minor-league character played by actor Kevin Costner in the movie *Bull Durham.* "He helps us at [Class AAA] Buffalo, gives us insurance at the big-league level, and he's a great influence on our young players. He is like having another coach."

Employed almost exclusively as a utility man who could play all the infield and outfield positions, as well as catcher, Manto obviously did not enjoy many highlights. His major-league career batting average was .230 with 31 home runs and 97 RBI. He does, however, share an all-time major-league record with 23 other players. In 1995, when he played for the Orioles, Manto hit home runs in four consecutive times at-bat over a three-game period (June 8-10). That was the season he delivered 17 homers in 254 trips to the plate in 89 games for Baltimore.

"I never spent a full year in the big leagues, not ever, which was discouraging except for the fact that I was getting paid every two

"Somebody asked me recently if I could speak in front of a small group of people and I said, 'Hey, I played and got booed in front of 45,000 people. What's the problem?'"

---

weeks for doing something I loved," said Manto. "I knew I had to either accept my role, whatever it was, or go home and find another way to earn a living, and I loved the game too much to give it up."

When he finally quit, Manto did so because "I was deflated. I had nothing left either mentally or physically. But I left happily, on my own terms."

While his four home runs in consecutive at-bats in 1995 always will be memorable, he stressed that the "real highlight" of his career came a year after he retired.

"It was in Buffalo in 2001 when they retired my uniform number [30]. They did it, they said, because of what I gave to them the years I played there. I was totally humbled, and it made everything I went through worthwhile."

Manto's signing bonus with the Angels in 1985 was $13,000. Three years earlier he'd been drafted by the Yankees but preferred a baseball scholarship to Temple University in Philadelphia, near his home in Bristol, Pennsylvania.

As for his highest salary in baseball, Manto said, "I don't know because I never spent a full year in the big leagues. On paper it would have been $410,000 [with Colorado in 2000], but I never got that much" because he was released early in the season.

"In the minors I made about 10 or 12 grand a month, and I got $800,000 in Japan [from the Yomiuri Giants in 1996] when they released me."

Manto and his wife, Denise, whom he married in 1993, have three children: Gabrielle, born in 1994, Andreana, in 1998, and Jeffrey, in 2000.

After ending his playing career, Manto coached and managed in the minor leagues for the Phillies from 2001 to 2002, and was the Pirates' roving minor-league hitting coordinator from 2003 to 2005, prior to his promotion as their batting coach.

When asked what is it that makes Manto a good hitting instructor for the Pirates, he said, "Because I know what it's like to be mediocre, what it feels like not to be good. I can help players because I went through it all myself. And because I did, I can get across to them how to play through heartache, what it takes to play through slumps."

On the subject of ongoing speculation concerning the use of performance-enhancing drugs by players, Manto was outspoken in his criticism. "It is unbelievable," he said. "Guys who are doing that have sold their souls to the devil for fame and money. It's not right.

"Not only is it wrong in terms of what it does to long-standing records established by guys like Babe Ruth and Hank Aaron and others, it's also wrong in terms of how bad steroids are for your health.

"Even if I thought that by taking steroids they would make me a major-league star, I would not do it. I would not sell my soul to the devil."

Of his long and often-discouraging career in baseball, spent mostly in minor-league towns, Manto insisted he had no complaints, no misgivings.

"If I had it to do over, I'd do it the same way. Absolutely. I have a lot of pride in what I did. I know how to work and how to get back up after being down. I know how to handle pressure because I played under pressure for 16 years.

"Somebody asked me recently if I could speak in front of a small group of people and I said, 'Hey, I played and got booed in front of 45,000 people. What's the problem?'

"I'm also proud of the way I am perceived, that people know, or should know you have to have some kind of strong character to put up with the kind of stuff I did for 16 years. Persistence and perseverance pays off. It's something you learn. When I started I didn't know what the heck to expect. It was always a dream, to have a long and successful career in the major leagues, but it always happened to somebody else.

"Until I got into professional baseball I had always been successful, but I never realized it because there never was a challenge. The first time I was challenged was when I went into professional baseball. I had always been the big guy, the guy who stood out in the team picture. Then came the challenge. It was persevere or go home. So I learned, and now here I am. Not a player anymore, now a batting coach. And happy to be one.

"But would I do anything different if I had my career to do all over again? No. I would not," Manto said again.

JACK
BROHAMER

Second Baseman, Third Baseman,
1972–75, 1980

Best season: 1974, 101 games,
.270 batting average, 2 home runs,
30 RBI

Indians career: 461 games,
.239 avg., 18 home runs, 125 RBI

He was called "Scrappy Jack" because that's the way Jack Brohamer played baseball for the Indians and two other teams during a nine-year major-league career.

It began when the Tribe picked Brohamer in the 34th round of the 1967 amateur draft and gave him a $1,000 signing bonus.

"It wasn't much, but it wasn't bad for a low-round draft choice, and besides, all I wanted was just a chance, that's all," Brohamer said from his home in Palm Desert, California.

"Ever since I was a little kid all I wanted to be was a baseball player," which he was as a professional for 14 years, including four in the minor leagues. But soon after his final season in his second tour of duty with the Indians in 1980, Brohamer launched another career that he found to be equally satisfying and, he said, even more rewarding than baseball in an emotional if not financial way.

As a detective sergeant with the Oceanside (California) Police Department until a few years ago, his job was investigating child molestation. "I dealt with young girls, most of them only seven or eight years old, and had to get them to tell me what happened, how they'd been abused and who molested them," said Brohamer.

"Later, when I'd see them in the hospital or their homes, they'd put their arms around me and, with tears in their eyes, thank me for helping them [prosecute the perpetrators]. That's what was especially rewarding . . . more than anything I'd ever done," said the former infielder, who earned his nickname in baseball despite his stature—165 pounds and 5 feet 10 inches tall (which always seemed to be at least a slight exaggeration).

"Scrappy Jack" had to give up police work in 1998 because of a ruptured disk in his back that required surgery and, since then, he is "almost" completely retired.

Almost, that is, since embarking upon what could be considered a third career—"sort of," he says—as a writer. It started in 2004.

"The editor of a local publication called *Desert Entertainer* asked if I'd be interested in writing a weekly column about golf," said Brohamer. "There are a lot of golf courses out here, and what I do is go around and play them, then write about them, rate them, things like that. It doesn't pay much money, but I have a lot of fun—and the perks are good because I can play the courses for nothing." He has a one handicap, though it took several years for him to completely recover from his back surgery.

Brohamer also does some part-time work for the Oceanside Police Department, conducting background investigations on applicants for employment. "I do just enough to keep me busy—as long as it doesn't interfere with my golf game," he said.

Brohamer and his wife, Helene, whom he married in 1967, raised two children, sons Jack and Greg.

After four seasons playing shortstop in the minor leagues, Brohamer was switched to second base and made it to the Indians in 1972. He was traded to the Chicago White Sox for whom he played in 1976 and 1977. He became a free agent and signed with Boston in 1978, and returned to Cleveland when the Tribe purchased his contract in mid-1980. He retired from baseball in 1981 when, at the end of spring training, he said, "I just walked away" after a bitter falling out with general manager Phil Seghi.

Among Brohamer's most pleasant memories in baseball were

"My heart is still with Cleveland, although it wasn't a very good organization when I played there. No money, for one thing."

_____

his two seasons with the White Sox, and he cited team owner Bill Veeck as one of the reasons. "Veeck asked me once, 'How much are we paying you?' and I told him, '$38,000,' and he said, 'Oh, that's not enough . . . I'm going to bump you up to $50,000,' which he did. How could you not like to play for a guy like that?"

The most he ever made in baseball, Brohamer said, was $100,000 one season as part of a three-year contract he signed as a free agent with the Red Sox.

It was during his 1977 season in Chicago that Brohamer experienced "the best thing I did in baseball. I went 5-for-5 and hit for the cycle on September 24 . . . the first White Sox player to do that since [Hall of Famer] Ray Schalk in 1922.

"Bob Lemon was the manager, and after I'd hit a homer, two doubles, and a single in four times at-bat, before I went to the plate the fifth time he told me, 'If you hit the ball, don't stop running until you get to third base,' and I didn't." It was a triple.

Despite his good times in Chicago, Brohamer said, "My heart is still with Cleveland, although it wasn't a very good organization when I played there. No money, for one thing, and other problems, too," he said without mentioning Seghi by name.

Among his most vivid—if not necessarily pleasant—memories of the Indians was in 1972 when he, then a rookie, made the team in spring training, only to learn that the season would not start on time because the Players Association was going on strike.

"We were in New Orleans for an exhibition game and [pitcher] Steve Mingori, then our player representative, called a team meeting to tell us we were going out on strike. Except that Steve sometimes had trouble saying what he meant. He said we were 'going on *stroke*,' and we all laughed our heads off, although it wasn't very funny. I guess we just didn't realize the seriousness of it. Anyway, then Ray Fosse took over and explained that we should just go home until we were called back. So Buddy Bell, Dick Tidrow, and I, all of us rookies then, piled into my car and headed to Cleveland. We had about $30 among us and . . ." Then he interjected, "Let me tell you something about Gaylord Perry [who had just been acquired by the Indians].

"No matter what anybody might say about Gaylord, he's the one guy who came to us and told us, 'If you guys need some money, just let me know. I'll give you what you need to make it wherever you're going.' Gaylord was the only one. Nobody else. A lot of guys didn't see that side of Gaylord. I did, and I never forgot it.

"Then, when we got about 50 miles outside of Cleveland, Buddy, who was driving, fell asleep, I think, hit the brake, and we spun around three or four times. Fortunately we were in the [grass] median and didn't hit anybody or roll over.

"A little while [13 days] later, after we got to Cleveland, the strike was settled and everything turned out all right."

But imagine what might have been the result if any or all three of the rookies had been injured—or worse—in the near-accident.

Nine-plus years later, in 1981, Brohamer, then a veteran, walked away from spring training ending his brief second career with the Indians and, as it turned out, his life in baseball.

"I would have liked to have been traded or to have caught on with another team, but it never happened. I'm not sure why. I could never prove it, but I don't think Seghi cared about helping me. Back then the teams had us [players] over a barrel. They had total control over us. Things were starting to change, but it took awhile.

"And now the pendulum has swung too far the other way, way too far. What's going on now is outlandish, with the salaries and all that's happening in baseball.

"You have to wonder—at least I do—where it's all going to end, and how it can continue the way things are going."

STEVE
MINGORI

Pitcher, 1970–73

Best season: 1971, 54 games,
1-2 won-lost record, 4 saves,
1.43 ERA

Indians career: 121 games,
2-8 won-lost record, 15 saves,
2.97 ERA

"I probably never would have gotten to Cleveland—or even made it to the big leagues—if it hadn't been for Alvin Dark," said Steve Mingori.

Mingori pitched in the major leagues for 10 seasons, the first three-plus with the Indians, from 1970 until June 8, 1973, when he was traded to Kansas City. He was with the Royals through 1979.

"I owe my major-league career to Dark," Mingori said of the oft-maligned former manager, who won and then lost an ugly power struggle with Gabe Paul during those chaotic days of Indians baseball in the 1960s and 1970s.

Mingori also credited Luis Isaac, who in 2006 was in his 42nd season in the Indians organization. Starting as a minor-league catcher in 1965, Isaac became a scout, minor league coach, manager, and, in 1998, the Tribe's bullpen coach.

Mingori, who still lives in Kansas City, Missouri, where he was born and raised, went on to coach for Toronto in the minor leagues for eight years, through 1994. He coached four more years in the Royals Baseball Academy and now gives private pitching lessons to aspiring young players.

"When you're sixty [as he was in 2004] and you've spent a big part of your life throwing a baseball as hard as you can, your body is like a used car, pretty much worn out and doesn't work so well," said Mingori.

He underwent major surgery on his neck on November 16, 2004. "It was very serious because, the doctor said, they had to deal with a lot of nerves. The nurse told me my neck was such a mess they had to treat it like I'd had a broken neck. I had pain down my leg, a burning sensation in my arm, and my shoulder hurt because everything in my neck had deteriorated.

"I always had pain when I was pitching, but in those days they gave you a couple of aspirins or a handful of pain pills—or even a greenie, which was legal then—or a shot of cortisone. Not like it is now. All along I thought my problem was a rotator cuff that I'd injured when I was pitching, but it turned out to be more than that.

"I was something of a freak. Even when I hurt, I could pitch six, seven days in a row. I could get warmed up with six pitches, and when I hurt, I'd pop a couple of pain pills and go out there again," he said. "As I said, things were different then . . . a lot different."

Mingori, twice divorced, is healed now after eight months in rehabilitation, and lives a quiet life. "I spend a lot of time with my three daughters: Mindy, who is a detective with the Kansas City police department; Cindy, who is married to a captain in the fire department; and Andrea, who is married to a motorcycle cop," he said.

Mingori, who was signed by Cincinnati as an amateur free agent in 1965, didn't make much progress in the Reds' minor-league system. But Dark saw him at Class AAA Indianapolis in 1969 and was impressed. Mingori was acquired by the Indians in a minor-league deal in February 1970. He was assigned to their Class AAA team in Wichita, Kansas, of the American Association.

"That's when Ken Aspromonte came into the picture," said Mingori. "He was the Wichita manager and, for whatever reason, we developed a personality conflict. I never understood why. We were both red-ass guys, but we also were paisanos [Italians] and should have gotten along better. But we didn't. Not ever.

"In spring training of 1970 in the Indians' minor-league camp, after I'd pitched batting practice one day, Dark invited me to work out with the big club, and then he had me pitch in a game against the Angels.

"Later he called me into his office. I was afraid he was going to send me home. Instead, he said he liked me, but that I needed another pitch to get right-handed hitters out, and told Isaac to teach me how to throw a screwball. I took it up and worked on it at Savannah [Class AA Southern League]. It was unbelievable! I got called up by the Indians in August, and the night I arrived in Cleveland, Dark put me in a game against the Yankees. It was my first chance in the big leagues. That's why I said I owe my career to Alvin Dark and Luis Isaac."

Mingori made 21 appearances the final two months, went 1-0, finished eight games, and was credited with one save. At that time the save rule was much more stringent; it was liberalized five years later.

But then, on July 30, 1971, Dark was fired and replaced by interim manager Johnny Lipon, and in 1972 Aspromonte was appointed manager of the Indians.

"Our personality conflict remained," said Mingori, even though in 1971 he appeared in 54 games with a 1-2 record and four saves. He was named "the best left-handed reliever in baseball" by the *Sporting News,* and Mingori's 1.43 earned run average was among the leaders in the big leagues.

"That also was the year *USA Today* ran a poll, and Carl Yastrzemski called me the toughest left-handed pitcher he faced, and Fred Lynn said I was the second toughest he faced. How about that?

"But I couldn't do anything right in Aspromonte's eyes. I was back and forth between [Class AAA] Portland and Cleveland the next season [1972]," during which he was 0-6 with 10 saves in 41 appearances.

"I have no idea why he hated me so much. I told him I wouldn't quit, that he should trade me if he didn't think I was any good, so he did."

———————————————

"It was more of the same in 1973 for me with the Indians, and between trips back and forth to the minor leagues. I pitched in only five games for Cleveland [without a decision], and in the middle of the season Aspromonte called me into his office and told me I should do my family a favor and quit baseball because I wasn't any good.

"I have no idea why he hated me so much. I told him I wouldn't quit, that he should trade me if he didn't think I was any good, so he did. A few days later [on June 8, 1973] I was dealt to Kansas City. I wasn't happy about it, but the way it turned out, it was Aspromonte who did my family and me the favor."

Mingori pitched through the 1979 season and ended his career with a won-lost record of 18-33, with a 3.03 earned run average and 42 saves in 385 major-league appearances.

"By then my arm was dead, though I got paid $90,000 in 1980, the second year of my two-year contract, the most I ever made in one season," he said.

With the Royals, Mingori pitched in three American League Championship Series, 1976–78, all of them against the New York Yankees, but never a World Series.

He made seven appearances in the three ALCS series and earned a save in Game 4 in 1976, though the Yankees won the pennant all three years.

But Mingori did get two World Series rings after launching his minor-league coaching career with the Toronto Blue Jays in 1987, which he continued through 1995. "I coached at every level and had some pretty good pitchers, but I never got back to the big leagues," he said.

Still, "When the Blue Jays won the World Series in 1992 and 1993, they gave all of their minor-league coaches and managers championship rings. It was a really nice gesture and greatly appreciated, even though it wasn't the same as helping them win it on the field."

After most of a lifetime in baseball—not as a superstar, nor even anything more than a now-and-then headline maker—Mingori has no regrets, only gratitude.

Especially for Alvin Dark and Luis Isaac for teaching him how to throw a screwball.

JACK
HEIDEMANN

Shortstop, 1969–72, 1974

Best season: 1970, 133 games, .211 batting average, 6 home runs, 37 RBI

Indians career: 239 games, .206 avg., 6 home runs, 46 RBI

"When I was young, all I wanted was to play in the big leagues," said Jack Heideman. "And when the Indians drafted me and I signed, I was the happiest kid around. But now that I'm old . . . well, not really old, but *older*, I realize that everything came too fast. Especially me making the team when I wasn't even 20."

Heidemann, a farm boy from Brenham, Texas, graduated from high school less than a month before the Indians selected him No. 1, 11th overall, in the 1967 amateur draft. They predicted he'd be "another Lou Boudreau." But it didn't happen.

Two years after the draft, Heidemann made it to the Indians in spring training, though his debut season consisted of only three games and three times at-bat (without a hit) before he was called to active duty for six months in the Texas Airborne National Guard.

Upon his return from the service in spring training, 1970, he became the Tribe's regular shortstop. The swift advancement pleased Heidemann.

However, his early promotion to the major leagues might have been—probably was, Heidemann now believes—the worst thing that could have happened to him.

"I could pick it [play shortstop], and I was a good hitter in high school and my first two years in the minor leagues," he said. "But I had no business being with the Indians that soon, facing pitchers like Baltimore had then—[Dave] McNally, [Jim] Palmer, [Pat] Dobson, [Mike] Cuellar. I was so overmatched it was unreal."

Heidemann lives in Mesa, Arizona, where he has been a real estate broker since his 1977 retirement from baseball. He and ex-wife Carol, whom he married in 1972, had two children: Michael, born in 1974, and Matthew in 1982. They adopted Jaime in 1985 and Molly in 1989. Heidemann never remarried.

"Michael had a chance to make it as a first baseman," Heidemann said of his oldest son. "I called him a 'white Willie McCovey,' but he got hurt diving for a ball, tore his rotator cuff when he was 21, and decided he was too old for surgery and to start all over again. He probably was right."

Heidemann spent parts of five seasons with the Tribe and went on to play for St. Louis (1974), New York Mets (1975–76), and Milwaukee (1976–77). He finished with a .211 career batting average in 426 major-league games over eight partial seasons. He also spent one year (1973) in the Oakland Athletics farm system—another aspect of his career for which he also harbors regret and resentment.

"I really believe I could have been something special, but I was just too young," he said. "It probably would have been better if I'd gone to a junior college for two years or accepted one of the [scholarship] offers I got from [the University of] Texas or Tulane. But I was just a kid back then. My dad was a farmer, my mom was a teacher, and we didn't have a lot of money.

"When the Indians drafted me, they flew me and my parents to Kansas City, where we negotiated my contract, though it wasn't really much of a negotiation. They offered [a signing bonus of] $27,000. We were going to ask for another $2,500, but then my dad said to me, 'Son, you want to play baseball?' Of course, I did. Then he said, 'Plus, they are going to pay you to play baseball. Is that right?' and I said yes again. So we signed. That was it.

"I just thought, and my dad thought the same, it was an opportunity for me to get off the farm, a chance that he'd never had."

In spring 1970, Heidemann was still considered a rookie with a promising future.

"Hawk Harrelson [then a Tribe outfielder] predicted I'd be the American League rookie of the year," said Heidemann.

But it didn't happen. The Yankees' Thurman Munson won in a landslide, receiving 23 of the 24 votes.

"I was disappointed, not because I didn't win, but that I didn't play as good as everybody expected," said Heidemann, who batted .211 in 133 games.

It didn't get any better in 1971. Heidemann suffered several injuries, starting with a strained shoulder in spring training. After the season began he was involved in a frightening collision with teammates John Lowenstein and Vada Pinson that hospitalized him for several days. And in September he hurt his knee and needed postseason surgery.

The operation was performed in Portland, Oregon, where Heidemann spent most of 1972 playing for the Indians' Class AAA farm club.

That also was the year he met and married Carol Cutler, the daughter of Bill Cutler, who was then president of the Pacific Coast League. Cutler previously had served as general manager of the Oakland Athletics, then owned by Charley Finley.

Heidemann's relationship with Cutler came into play and proved detrimental to Heidemann in 1973 after he was traded to Oakland with Ray Fosse for Dave Duncan and George Hendrick.

The A's immediately sent Heidemann to Class AAA Tucson, and when he received a contract from Finley calling for a large cut in salary, he refused to sign.

"Finley told me, 'Son, sign the contract or get another job,'" related Heidemann. "When I finally did sign, Finley said, 'By the way, tell your father-in-law I said hello.'"

It was Finley's not-so-subtle way of sticking it to Cutler, who had

"I enjoy watching baseball, but the financial aspect is a shame . . . everything is out of whack and getting worse. A man can't take his family to many games because it costs too much."

sued Finley and won a large judgment after the two men had a falling out over Cutler's termination.

The Indians re-acquired Heidemann, purchasing his contract from the A's on March 25, 1974, obviously in the hope that the 24-year-old shortstop would regain the promise he'd shown as a high school kid and minor leaguer. But again it didn't happen, and two months later he was dealt to the Cardinals. Heidemann spent 1975 and part of 1976 with the Mets, played for the Brewers through 1977, and agreed to a demotion to Class AAA Spokane in 1978.

"The Brewers told me," said Heidemann, "'We've got a kid we want to give a shot, and if we need you, we'll get you.'"

That "kid" was Paul Molitor—the same Paul Molitor who went on to play 21 years in the major leagues, compiled a .306 career batting average, and was elected to the Baseball Hall of Fame in 2004.

Heidemann returned to Spokane in 1979 but suffered another injury, this one to his rotator cuff, and missed most of the season. "When it was over, I knew my time was up. I said goodbye to baseball and never looked back."

But then he did look back, recalling his biggest thrill in the game, providing even more insight into the personality of the once overawed farm boy from Brenham.

"It was the first time we went into Yankee Stadium," he said. "I stood at home plate and thought, 'Here I am, little Jackie Heidemann from Brenham High School standing where Babe Ruth and Mickey Mantle and Roger Maris and Casey Stengel and all the guys I had worshipped had played.'"

And now that he's "not really old, but *older*," what are his thoughts on the game today? "I enjoy watching baseball, but the financial aspect is a shame. I don't mind the owners making a lot of money, and I don't mind the players making a lot of money. But everything is out of whack and getting worse. A man can't take his family to many games because it costs too much. Everything is just too darned expensive.

"The most I made in baseball was $42,500 in 1976, which I thought was pretty good. But what's happening now is unreal. You tell kids what it was like when I was their age, and they think you're either lying or crazy."

And when Heidemann was their age, one month out of high school in 1967, all he ever wanted was to play in the major leagues, which he did, and was thrilled to do so.

Except that—as he knows now—it all happened too soon.

MIKE
PAUL

Pitcher, 1968–71

Best season: 1969, 47 games, 5-10 won-lost record, 2 saves, 3.61 ERA

Indians career: 130 games, 14-33 won-lost record, 5 saves, 4.39 ERA

You'll not find a bust of Mike Paul in the Baseball Hall of Fame, nor even his name on a ballot, but that's not to demean the former left-handed pitcher whose resume is much richer than his record.

Few men have been involved in baseball as much or as long as Paul. His obvious love for the game is manifested by the length and variety of jobs he's held since ending his major-league pitching career in 1974.

"I've always enjoyed being part of the game, no matter where or whatever level, as a player, coach, and now as an advance scout," said Paul, who was on the payroll of the Colorado Rockies in 2006, his 39th consecutive year—and counting—in professional baseball.

Certainly, there's more glamour—and more money—in being in uniform and, of course, logging time in the major-league baseball players' pension plan. But even that doesn't change Paul's thinking. He already is vested with eight years of service time, a little shy of the 10 needed for maximum benefits.

"The way I look at it," he said, "if I were back in uniform [as a coach], it'd mean dealing with 25 different guys and maybe not liking 20 of them, but still having to put up with them. This way I can pick my own friends. As long as it's baseball, I'm happy.

"And during the off season all I have to do is make sure I hit my drives straight, and then do some chipping and putting. During the winter, my time is my own."

Paul was a low round 20th-round draft choice of the Indians in 1967. He was 22 years old and had just helped the University of Arizona reach the College World Series in 1966. He received a signing bonus of "all of $500 to pay my college bills," as he said, and made it to the Indians in less than two seasons in the minor leagues.

"In the beginning I was strictly a starter. But after I got to Cleveland and we had Sam McDowell, Luis Tiant, Sonny Siebert, and Steve Hargan, as well as Stan Williams, you had to be very good to break into that rotation, and I wasn't *that* good," said Paul. He was relegated to the bullpen.

Again, no disrespect intended, Paul was never a big star but did well in his role as a spot-starter and reliever—and one-time first baseman—for the Tribe through 1971, then for Texas (1972–73) and the Chicago Cubs (1973–74). It was with the Cubs in 1974 that Paul made $33,000, his largest major-league salary.

"That was before the advent of free agency. I played winter ball every year to make ends meet," he said.

After he "retired" from the major leagues, Paul played eight more seasons in the Mexican League.

Eddie Leon, Paul's former teammate in college and with the Indians, recommended him to Mexico and vice versa in 1975. It launched a second playing career for Paul, first at Tampico, where he pitched through 1976, then at Juarez from 1977 to 1981, and finally with the Mexico City Reds in 1982.

"The money wasn't bad. I made between $28,000 and $32,000 [a season] in Mexico," said Paul. "It was better than I could do in Triple-A, and it was tax-free."

As did Leon in another story in this book, Paul said that baseball in Mexico is played much differently than baseball in the major leagues—and then he said again, "but it's *still* baseball."

Perhaps the largest difference, according to Paul, was an especially "hilarious" experience playing in Tampico, primarily because of the peculiarity of its ball park.

"Believe it or not—which I didn't at first—a railroad track runs right across the outfield. Every night at a certain time on schedule the game was held up to allow a train to pass through.

"I had played winter ball in Mexico previously, so I was aware of the conditions, and how every player had to provide his own undershirt, sanitary socks, and towel. But I never saw anything like a train running through the outfield at Tampico every night.

"It wasn't all bad, but after two seasons I was thinking about quitting and going back to the States to try to play again in the big leagues. I told the [Tampico] owner my arm was tired, and I shut it down for the last two weeks of the season. And with that he traded me to Juarez, which is right across the Rio Grande from El Paso, and all of a sudden my arm got real strong," said Paul.

"Juarez is a great place to play. I pitched there for five years, made decent money, and lived in El Paso. I was still a Gringo, but I wasn't a dumb Gringo. All I had to do was drive back and forth across the border for games, which was no problem."

El Paso also was only about five hours from Paul's home in Tucson, Arizona, where he and his wife, Rosalie, whom he married in 1969, raised two daughters, Amanda, born in 1977, and Allison, in 1980.

"After five seasons for Juarez—five pretty good seasons for me—I got traded to Mexico City [in 1982] where it's like playing in New York. The fans are very excitable and, if you won, they love you. But if you lost . . . well, then they didn't even like you.

"I hung it up after one year. The peso had been devalued and I was 38, so Rosalie and I felt it was time to go home."

Paul said he had a couple of 20-win seasons in Mexico, and that his career record there was 104-56, a .615 winning percentage, with a 2.06 earned run average in 1,434 innings.

Since returning to the U.S., Paul was the Class A minor-league pitching coach for San Diego in 1983 and 1984; Class AAA minor-league pitching coach for Milwaukee in 1985 and 1986; bullpen coach for the Oakland Athletics under Tony LaRussa in 1987 and 1988; pitching coach for the Seattle Mariners from 1989 to 1991; the Athletics' advance scout in 1992 and 1994, and their bench coach in 1993; advance scout for Texas from 1995 to 2001; advance scout for the Chicago Cubs in 2002; advance scout for the Arizona Diamondbacks in 2003 and 2004, and advance scout for the Washington Nationals in 2005, before joining the Colorado Rockies as their advance scout in 2006.

Paul underwent rotator cuff surgery in 1998 for an arm injury he suffered (but which was never correctly diagnosed) when he pitched for the Indians, making even more remarkable the nearly 1,500 innings he pitched in Mexico in his eight-year second career.

As for his previously being mentioned as a one-time first baseman, that happened in 1968 in a game in Detroit. "We were in the eighth or ninth inning, I was pitching in relief, and a tough, right-handed hitter was the next batter," said Paul.

"Alvin Dark came to the mound and said he wanted me to go play first base. I said, 'What?' And he said, 'I want you to play first base for one hitter while I bring in Stan Williams. Then I'll bring you back in to face Jim Northrup or one of their other left-handed batters.'

"So there I was, standing at first base, and Emmett Ashford, the umpire, said to me, 'Mike, make sure you keep your foot on the base.' I told him, 'Emmett, I just hope they hit a fly ball.' I was just a rookie and I was flat-out scared I was going to screw up.

"The batter got a hit, and that was it. I went back to the mound and, because Dark had taken out Tony Horton for me to play first base, we didn't have another first baseman. Lee Maye, an outfielder, had to go to first base—and you can imagine what happened.

"Northrup hit my first pitch on the ground to Maye; he botched it, and we lost. It's like they always say, you can't hide somebody who's playing out of position . . . the ball will find him.

"I'm just glad it didn't find me."

DOUG
JONES

Relief Pitcher, 1986–91, 1998

Best season: 1990, 66 games,
5-5 won-lost record, 43 saves,
2.56 ERA

Indians career: 295 games,
27-34 won-lost record, 129 saves,
3.06 ERA

It was perseverance, rather than a blazing fastball, that made it possible for Doug Jones to pitch 16 years in the major leagues. He toiled for parts of nine seasons in the minors before becoming one of the most successful relief pitchers in the history of baseball.

In 1978, when he was selected in the third round of the supplemental amateur draft by Milwaukee, few among baseball's talent sleuths thought Jones threw hard enough to pitch in the big leagues. The Brewers picked him on the strength of the success he'd enjoyed as a starting pitcher at Central Arizona Junior College. They gave him what Jones called "a minimal bonus . . . let me just say it was less than $5,000," which, in reality, meant the Brewers considered him to be a possible "project," as opposed to a "prospect."

Even Jones admits that when he was a starter in the Brewers' minor-league system from 1978 to 1984, "I threw just about everything in the book—fastball, curve, slider—though none of them was very good, except that I could throw them all for strikes. And I don't mean batting-practice strikes, or just throwing the ball over the plate. I mean throwing them where I wanted them, for strikes."

But it didn't get him anywhere, at least not with the Brewers, who gave him a perfunctory trial—four appearances for a total of

2⅔ innings—in the big leagues in 1982. They released him at the end of the 1984 season after he'd pitched with only moderate success for six minor-league teams, compiling an undistinguished 48-48 record over seven seasons.

"I was going on 27, and I guess they thought I was getting too old," said Jones.

And, of course, the Brewers also thought he didn't throw hard enough, that his fastball wasn't fast enough.

Despite the rejection, Jones refused to quit.

"For one thing, I couldn't go home [at that time to Lebanon, Indiana] and earn a good living because I wasn't qualified to do much," he said. "Besides, I loved the game, I loved to pitch—I still thought I could be successful—and I wanted to continue playing.

"I called around to see if any club needed a warm body who could throw strikes. Jim Napier [the Indians' director of player development] told me, 'C'mon down [to Tucson] and show us what you've got.'"

Jones did—at his own expense for three weeks—and finally the Indians signed him to a minor-league contract. That's when he went to the bullpen full time, at Class AA Waterbury (Connecticut) in 1985, and Class AAA Maine in 1986.

It's also when Jones perfected a pitch he'd picked up earlier. It's called a "circle change" and has been described as "something like a screwball." Basically, it's an off-speed pitch that looks like a fastball without great velocity, and it breaks down and in on a right-handed batter, down and away to a left-hander.

"The main thing, I threw strikes. If you walk people or can't throw the ball where you want it, you can't be successful. You have to make the batter swing the bat, make him know he has to swing the bat to get on base," he said, sounding very much like a pitching coach, which he indicated he'd like to be if the right opportunity presents itself.

Throwing strikes and changing speeds earned him a promotion to the Indians in September 1986, and this one was not limited to a 2⅔-inning trial as had been the case with the Brewers in 1982.

"After I got up with the Indians, I threw all my pitches—both of them, fastballs and change-ups—for strikes."

When asked how hard he threw, Jones said, "I think my best fastball was in the mid-80s [mph]. I never threw harder, and my change-up was in the 65 to 75 range."

Now living in Tucson, Arizona, Jones and his wife, Debbie, whom he married in 1982, have three sons: Dustin, born in 1984, Dylan in 1989, and Dawson in 1992. All of them, their father said, are "good enough to play any sport they put their mind to," which was the attitude that Jones himself embraced in his 23-year professional baseball odyssey.

He arrived in Cleveland in September of 1986 after two seasons in the Tribe farm system. In recalling his status at that time, Jones indicated that not everyone within the organization agreed that he belonged at the major-league level.

"When I got called up, I don't think my pitching style was very popular," he said. "There were several individuals who thought that a pitcher who didn't throw any harder than I did didn't belong in the major leagues. It's not necessary to say who they were because it doesn't matter now.

"The fact is, that [still] seems to be the prevailing mentality in baseball. If you are a pitcher and you don't throw over 90, they [scouts] might not even bother talking to you."

Of his time with the Indians, Jones said, "They were trying to put a winner on the field and didn't have anybody else to put out there. That's probably the reason I got to play, because they didn't have anybody who could throw 90 or 91, other than Ernie Camacho, but he wasn't very successful."

That's when Jones inherited the closer's job, and thrived in it.

"I loved it in Cleveland. I had a great time. I was doing well, though I was frustrated that we couldn't put together the whole package. A couple of years we were scoring as many runs as anybody in baseball, but we couldn't stop the other team, either defensively or with pitching. We were short in both of those areas, off and on."

With the exception of a two-month stint in 1987 when he was

sent back to Class AAA Buffalo, Jones was in the big leagues to stay—with the Indians through 1991 (and again in 1998), Houston (1992–93), Philadelphia (1994), Baltimore (1995), Chicago Cubs (1996), Milwaukee (1996–98), and Oakland (1999–2000).

In his final season with the Athletics, Jones—at the age of 43—appeared in 54 games. His four victories in six decisions with two saves gave him a statistical bottom line of 1,128⅓ innings pitched in 846 games with 303 saves, 69 victories, 79 losses, and a 3.71 earned run average for 16 major-league seasons.

Those 303 saves at the time ranked 18th on the all-time list headed by Lee Smith with 478.

Jones's best years were with the Indians, especially 1988–90 when he was credited with 37, 32, and 43 saves, respectively, for a three-season total of 112.

In his six-plus years with the Tribe, Jones set a club record of 129 saves. It stood until May 7, 2006, when Bob Wickman was credited with his 130th save since coming to Cleveland on July 28, 2000.

Jones was elected the Indians' Man of the Year in 1988 and again in 1990, and represented the Tribe on the American League all-star team three times (1988–90). He was credited with the save in the A.L.'s 5-3 victory in 1989, and in 1994, when he was with Philadelphia, Jones was the winning pitcher in the National League's 8-7 victory. It was his fifth All-Star Game appearance.

His largest salary was $2.875 million when he played for the Phillies. He earned $2.05 million with the Indians in 1991. All of which was pretty good for a guy who went from being in limbo—when nobody in baseball thought he was good enough because he didn't throw hard enough—to become one of the all-time best relievers in history because, as said, "I threw strikes."

And also because he refused to accept rejection—and persevered because he loved the game and, especially, because he loved to pitch.

Cleveland Guides & Gifts
More good books from Gray & Company

Try one of these other great books about Cleveland . . .

SPORTS

Heart of a Mule / Former Browns and OSU Buckeye player, Dick Schafrath retells many wild and entertaining stories from his life. *Dick Schafrath* / $24.95 hardcover

Dealing / A rare behind-the-scenes look at the Cleveland Indians front office that will provide insight to many Indians fans. *Terry Pluto* / $24.95 hardcover

Best of Hal Lebovitz / A collection of great sportswriting from six decades, by the late dean of Cleveland sportswriters. *Hal Lebovitz* / $14.95 softcover

Cleveland Sports Legends / The 20 most glorious & gut-wrenching moments in Cleveland sports history. *Bob Dyer* / $24.95 hardcover

Curses! Why Cleveland Sports Fans Deserve to Be Miserable / A collection of a lifetime of tough luck, bad breaks, goofs, gaffes, and blunders. *Tim Long* / $9.95 softcover

On Being Brown / Essays and interviews ponder what it means to be a true Browns fan. *Scott Huler* / $12.95 softcover

Browns Town 1964 / The remarkable story of the upstart AFC Cleveland Browns' surprise championship win over the hugely favored Baltimore Colts. *Terry Pluto* / $14.95 softcover

False Start / A top sportswriter looks at how the new Browns were set up to fail. *Terry Pluto* / $19.95 hardcover

The Toe / No one played longer for the Browns. Relive the golden era of pro football in this autobiography by Lou "The Toe" Groza. *with Mark Hodermarsky* / $12.95 softcover

Heroes, Scamps & Good Guys / 101 profiles of the most colorful characters from Cleveland sports history. Will rekindle memories for any Cleveland sports fan. *Bob Dolgan* / $24.95 hardcover

The View from Pluto / Award-winning sportswriter Terry Pluto's best columns about Northeast Ohio sports from 1990–2002. *Terry Pluto* / $14.95 softcover

LeBron James / From high school hoops to #1 NBA draft pick, an inside look at the rise of basketball's hottest young star. *David Lee Morgan, Jr.* / $14.95 softcover

Our Tribe / A father, a son, and the relationship they shared through their mutual devotion to the Cleveland Indians. *Terry Pluto* / $14.95 softcover

Omar! / All-Star shortstop Omar Vizquel retells his life story on and off the field in this candid baseball memoir. Includes 41 color photos. *With Bob Dyer* / $14.95 softcover

Cleveland Golfer's Bible / All of Greater Cleveland's golf courses and driving ranges described in detail. Essential guide for any golfer. *John H. Tidyman* / $13.95 softcover

Golf Getaways from Cleveland / 50 great golf trips just a short car ride from home. Plan easy weekends, business meetings, reunions, other gatherings. *John H. Tidyman* / $14.95 softcover

TRAVEL & GUIDES

Ohio Road Trips / Discover 52 of Neil Zurcher's all-time favorite Ohio getaways. *Neil Zurcher* / $13.95 softcover

Cleveland Ethnic Eats / The guide to authentic ethnic restaurants and markets in Northeast Ohio. *Laura Taxel* / $13.95 softcover

52 Romantic Outings in Greater Cleveland / Easy-to-follow "recipes" for romance —a lunch hour, an evening, or a full day together. *Miriam Carey* / $13.95 softcover

Great Inn Getaways from Cleveland / 58 distinctive inns & hotels perfect for a weekend or an evening away from home. *Doris Larson* / $14.95 softcover

Bed & Breakfast Getaways from Cleveland / 80 charming small inns, perfect for an easy weekend or evening away from home. *Doris Larson* / $14.95 softcover

Ohio Oddities / An armchair guide to the offbeat, way out, wacky, oddball, and otherwise curious roadside attractions of the Buckeye State. *Neil Zurcher* / $13.95 softcover

Continued . . .

Cleveland Cemeteries / Meet Cleveland's most interesting "permanent" residents in these 61 outdoor history parks. *Vicki Blum Vigil* / $13.95 softcover

Cleveland on Foot / Beyond Cleveland on Foot / Great hikes and self-guided walking tours in and around Greater Cleveland and 7 neighboring counties. *Patience Cameron Hoskins, with Rob & Peg Bobel* / $15.95 (each) softcover

HISTORY & NOSTALGIA

Strange Tales from Ohio / Offbeat tales about the Buckeye State's most remarkable people, places, and events. *Neil Zurcher* / $13.95 softcover

Cleveland Food Memories / A nostalgic look back at the food we loved, the places we bought it, and the people who made it special. *Gail Ghetia Bellamy* / $17.95 softcover

Cleveland Amusement Park Memories / A nostalgic look back at Euclid Beach Park, Puritas Springs Park, Geauga Lake Park, and other classic parks. *David & Diane Francis* / $19.95 softcover

Cleveland Cops / A collection of the real stories cops tell each other. *John H. Tidyman* / $24.95 hardcover

Ghoulardi / The behind-the-scenes story of Cleveland's wildest TV legend. Rare photos, interviews, show transcripts, and Ghoulardi trivia. *Tom Feran & R. D. Heldenfels* / $17.95 softcover

Barnaby and Me / Linn Sheldon, a Cleveland TV legend as "Barnaby," tells the fascinating story of his own extraordinary life. / $12.95 softcover

The Cleveland Orchestra Story / How a midwestern orchestra became a titan in the world of classical music. With 102 rare photographs. *Donald Rosenberg* / $40.00 hardcover

Finding Your Family History / Practical how-to with detailed instructions to help find the roots to your family tree in Northeast Ohio. *Vicki Blum Vigil* / $19.95 softcover

Whatever Happened to the "Paper Rex" Man? / Nostalgic essays and photos rekindle memories of Cleveland's Near West Side neighborhood. *The May Dugan Center* / $15.95 softcover

CRIME & MYSTERY

The Milan Jacovich mystery series / Cleveland's favorite private eye solves tough cases in these 9 popular detective novels. *Les Roberts* / $13.95 (each) softcover

We'll Always Have Cleveland / The memoir of mystery novelist Les Roberts, his character Milan Jacovich, and the city of Cleveland. *Les Roberts* / $24.95 hardcover

Women Behaving Badly / 16 strange-but-true tales of Cleveland's most ferocious female killers. *John Stark Bellamy II* / $24.95 hardcover

They Died Crawling / The Maniac in the Bushes / The Corpse in the Cellar / The Killer in the Attic / Death Ride at Euclid Beach / Five collections of gripping true tales about notable Cleveland crimes and disasters. Includes photos. / $13.95 softcover (each)

AND MUCH MORE . . .

Cleveland: A Portrait of the City / 105 color photographs capture Greater Cleveland's landmarks and hidden details in all seasons. *Jonathan Wayne* / $35.00 hardcover

Full of It / Strong words and fresh thinking for Cleveland, by *Plain Dealer* columnist Sam Fulwood. *Sam Fulwood III* / $24.95 hardcover

Is It Just Me? / Columnist Dick Feagler pulls no punches in this collection of hard-hitting *Plain Dealer* columns. / $24.95 hardcover

"I know I'm not supposed to say this . . . But I'll say it anyway." / More controversial recent columns by Dick Feagler, dean of Cleveland newspaper columnists. / $22.95 hardcover

Feagler's Cleveland / "Did You Read Feagler Today?" / The best and most talked about columns from three decades of commentary by Cleveland's top columnist, Dick Feagler. / $13.95 softcover (each)

Faith and You / 28 short essays on finding faith to face each day and trying to live that day the right way. *Terry Pluto* / $19.95 hardcover

Everyday Faith / Practical essays on personal faith and the ethical choices we face in everyday life. *Terry Pluto* / $19.95 hardcover

Available from Northeast Ohio bookstores and most online booksellers.
Or order from any bookstore, anywhere. Questions? **Call us toll-free: 1-800-915-3609.**

Gray & Company, Publishers · Cleveland · www.grayco.com